Service Purchasing: What Every Buyer Should Know

LeRoy H. Graw
C.P.M., CPCM, EdD

Deidre M. Maples
M.B.A.

VNR VAN NOSTRAND REINHOLD
_____ New York

134953

Copyright © 1994 by Van Nostrand Reinhold

Library of Congress Catalog Card Number 93-10225
ISBN 0-442-01718-9

All rights reserved. No part of this work covered by
the copyright hereon may be reproduced or used in any
form or by any means—graphic, electronic, or
mechanical, including photocopying, recording, taping,
or information storage and retrieval systems—without
the written permission of the publisher.

I(T)P Van Nostrand Reinhold is an International Thomson Publishing company.
ITP logo is a trademark under license.

Printed in the United States of America.

Van Nostrand Reinhold   International Thomson Publishing GmbH
115 Fifth Avenue   Königswinterer Str. 518
New York, New York 10003   5300 Bonn 3
                                         Germany

International Thomson Publishing
Berkshire House, 168-173   International Thomson Publishing Asia
High Holborn   38 Kim Tian Rd., #0105
London WC1V 7AA   Kim Tian Plaza
England   Singapore 0316

Thomas Nelson Australia   International Thomson Publishing Japan
102 Dodds Street   Kyowa Building, 3F
South Melbourne 3205   2-2-1 Hirakawacho
Victoria, Australia   Chiyada-Ku, Tokyo 102
                                         Japan

Nelson Canada
1120 Birchmount Road
Scarborough, Ontario
M1K 5G4, Canada

16 15 14 13 12 11 10 9 8 7 6 5 4 3 2 1

Library of Congress Cataloging-in-Publication Data

Graw, LeRoy H.
    Service purchasing : what every buyer should know / LeRoy H. Graw,
Deidre M. Maples.
        p.   cm.
    Includes bibliographical references and index.
    ISBN 0-442-01718-9
    1. Service industries—Management.   2. Industrial procurement.
    I. Maples, Deidre M.   II. Title.
    HD9980.5.G7   1993
    658.7′2—dc20
                                                         93-10225
                                                            CIP

To our spouses, Wayne Maples and Anat Graw,
and to our children, Megan Maples, Byron Graw,
and Karen Graw.

Contents

Introduction   **xi**

Chapter 1   **What is a Service? Purchasing Services
Versus Purchasing Supplies   1**

DEFINING AND CATEGORIZING SERVICES   1
DIFFERENCES BETWEEN SUPPLY AND SERVICE
   PURCHASING   5
SUMMARY   14

Chapter 2   **The Advance Purchasing Planning Process
for Services   17**

THE ADVANCE PURCHASING PLAN AS A BASIS
   FOR SUPPLIER SELECTION   17
GUIDELINES FOR TEMPORARY SERVICE
   CONTRACTING   21
SUMMARY   22

Chapter 3   **The Service Contract Statement of Work   25**

GENERAL SCOPE OF WORK   25
DOCUMENTS AND REFERENCES   26
EXPLICIT REQUIREMENTS   26

134453

PROGRESS REPORTS   26
SUMMARY   28

Chapter 4   Contract Types Appropriate for Services   31

CONTRACT TYPES   33
SUMMARY   46

Chapter 5   The Service Contract Solicitation   49

ELEMENTS OF THE SOLICITATION   49
SUMMARY   59

Chapter 6   The Service Contract Evaluation and Selection Process   61

PRICE ANALYSIS   62
COST ANALYSIS   63
NONPRICE SELECTION CRITERIA (BEST-VALUE SOURCE SELECTION)   64
SUMMARY   74

Chapter 7   Negotiating and Awarding the Service Contract   77

STEPS IN THE NEGOTIATION PROCESS   77
AWARDING THE CONTRACT   82
DEALING WITH UNSUCCESSFUL OFFERORS   83
NOTICE TO PROCEED   83
SUMMARY   84

Chapter 8   Service Contract Administration   87

ROUTINE VERSUS NONROUTINE CONTRACT ADMINISTRATION   87
THE CONTRACT ADMINISTRATION TEAM   88
PLANNING FOR CONTRACT ADMINISTRATION   91
ORDERING AND WORK AUTHORIZATION   93
NEGOTIATING CHANGES TO CONTRACTS   96
EXERCISING RENEWAL OPTIONS IN SERVICE CONTRACTS   105
SUMMARY   115

Chapter 9   Claims, Terminations, and Disputes   119

DIFFERING SITE CONDITIONS AND
   SUSPENSIONS OF WORK   119
CLAIMS AVOIDANCE   120
TERMINATIONS   124
DISPUTES   127
SUMMARY   128

**Chapter 10   Evaluating Supplier Performance and Closing
Out Contracts   131**

SERVICE SUPPLIER PERFORMANCE
   EVALUATIONS   131
CLOSEOUTS OF SERVICE CONTRACTS   131
SUMMARY   132
CONCLUSION   132

References   135

Appendix A   The Service Contract Act   139

**Appendix B   Laws Governing Public Sector Construction
Contracting   143**

Appendix C   Work Words   147

Appendix D   Ambiguous Terms   149

**Appendix E   Description/Specification/Work
Statement   151**

Appendix F   Example Request for Quotation   165

Appendix G   Example Contract Agreement   171

Appendix H   The Contract Administration Team   175

**Appendix I   Work Order and Payment Procedures Flow Chart
for an Indefinite-Delivery Type Contract   177**

Appendix J   Contract Closeout Checklist   179

Index   183

Introduction

Strictly speaking, service purchasing is the act of purchasing a service. Effective service purchasing entails the following:

1. having the right actions performed at the right place, at the right time, for the right price;
2. ensuring performance quality; and
3. maintaining records of which suppliers performed well.

Such statements are deceptively simple.

In many circumstances effective purchasing can truly be relatively simple. Low dollar purchases, for example, do not justify the time and talent required to make careful, complex judgments and perform sophisticated purchasing procedures. High dollar, complex purchases, on the other hand, require such time and talent if the organization is to be effective and competitive in the marketplace.

An effective, competitive organization must perform all of its tasks well. Such tasks include the core activity (whatever that might be); administration; marketing; accounting/finance; and obtaining the proper facilities, services, materials, and supplies. In a very real sense, it does not matter whether the core activity is manufacturing, a service, or even governmental in nature. The organization can be no better than the inputs it uses to perform its tasks, whatever they are: Garbage-In-Garbage-Out, to steal a phrase.

For many years resources in the United States were plentiful and therefore cheap. Little care was needed to secure the proper inputs to perform well. In a shrinking world, with the importance of global markets and the level of competition increasing, this is no longer the case.

Progressive organizations now realize the importance of effective purchasing. The high degree of problem-solving ability and training required to perform more complex purchasing tasks is becoming more widely recognized. Effective purchasing of all input types is necessary, for example, to implement such quality programs as Total Quality Control, Total Quality Management, and World-Class Manufacturing. Today's marketplace recognizes that increasing quality can decrease costs by implementing quality concepts in all phases of the organization, including purchasing. High-quality purchasing permits the organization to acquire high-quality inputs for costs that permit the firm to be competitive.

High-quality purchasing involves the ability to make such sophisticated strategic decisions as whether it is better under the prevailing circumstances to partner with a supplier, or engage in arms-length negotiations. It also involves the ability to perform complex tactical functions such as cost and profit analysis.

Purchasing services, if done properly, generally falls in the category of complex purchases. Organizations generally purchase those services they view as being one-of-a-kind. From the buyer's point of view, building a shopping center is likely to be more individualistic than buying pencils, or even railroad cars. Although the construction company may have built many shopping centers, the investors paying for the work are probably not buying shopping centers in bulk; if they were, they would buy the construction company.

Services purchased outside the firm can also be quite expensive. Neither auditors nor construction companies work cheap. The complexity, individualistic nature, and expense of service purchases result in the need to invest more time and talent to ensure the purchase is done right.

In many ways purchasing services differs from purchasing supplies, although experience gained in purchasing supplies can be transferred to purchasing services. This book is written to acquaint purchasing professionals with underlying concepts, practices, and procedures in the specialized area of service purchasing. It will:

1. define services;
2. highlight the differences between supply and service purchasing;
3. explain the process used to locate and identify potential service suppliers;
4. explain how to prepare effective statements of work for services;
5. describe the solicitation, evaluation, selection, and award processes for service suppliers;
6. describe how to structure an effective service contract;

7. explain the procedures used to monitor performance of service suppliers; and
8. explain the procedures used to evaluate performance of service-supplier performance.

This is a hands-on, nuts-and-bolts book on service purchasing methodology. It is designed to help the purchasing practitioner perform effectively in a difficult area and to help the organization obtain the desired quality of service for a good price, thus attaining competitive excellence.

Service Purchasing: What Every Buyer Should Know

1

What is a Service? Purchasing Services Versus Purchasing Supplies

DEFINING AND CATEGORIZING SERVICES

Defining the term "Service" in the purchasing context is not as simple as it might at first seem. A review of six authorities (Aljian's (1982); Dobler, Lee, and Burt (1984); Kendrick (1986); the Standard Industrial Classification Manual (1987); the Federal Acquisition Regulation (1992); and the Office of Federal Procurement Policy Proposed Policy Letter 92 (1991)) yielded six different definitions. None was well suited for use in a wide variety of organizations. The range of possible services is extremely broad, but most organizations need only part of that total. Further, there are distinctive patterns of service needs for different types of organizations. A comprehensive definition of services in the purchasing context should not only include the broad array of services, but should also recognize the purchasing patterns of different organizational types.

The Aljian's (1982) definition in Table 1-1 includes services found in most commercial/industrial settings. It does not include several types of services often contracted for in the public sector. Examples of such services include research and development (R&D); services relating to the maintenance, repair, and operation of buildings; and utilities services.

The Kendrick (1986) definition in Table 1-2 reflects the thinking of the average consumer rather than the buyer of organizational services.

The Dobler, Lee, and Burt (1984) definition in Table 1-3 reflects a broad cross section of services purchased by most organizations, but omits the facilities-related services that many organizations purchase. The fifth edition (and most recent) of this commonly used purchasing text did not provide any succinct classification system for services.

TABLE 1-1   Service industry definitions according to ALJIAN'S.

Professional services: Legal, engineering, architectural, data processing, programming, testing, consulting, temporary employees, and so forth.

Facilities and equipment-related services: Janitorial, equipment maintenance, security, data processing, reproduction, and so forth.

Personnel-related services: Clothing and employee personal articles, vending machines, and so forth.

Labor and craft services: Construction.

Source: George W. Aljian and Paul V. Farrell. *Aljian's Purchasing Handbook*, 4th ed. (New York: McGraw-Hill Book Company, 1982).

TABLE 1-2   Service industry definitions according to KENDRICK.

Transportation: Railroads, subways, airlines, bus lines, common carrier, trucking, and pipelines.

Public utilities: Telephone communications, energy services, sanitation services.

Restaurants, hotels, and motels

Retail: Food, apparel, automotive, wholesale trade, department stores.

Real estate

News media

Personal services: Amusements, laundry and cleaning, barber and beauty shops.

Professional services: Lawyers, doctors, and so forth.

Government: Defense, health, education, welfare and municipal services.

Source: John L. Kendrick, "The Service Industries' Tools." *Quality* (October 1986): p. 13.

TABLE 1-3   Service categories according to Dobler, Lee, and Burt.

Personal services: Consulting, engineering, technical, medical, training and education, auctioneering, arbitration, and temporary employee services.

Equipment and processing services: Maintenance, overhaul, servicing, modernization, salvage, data processing, photographic, printing, publication, housekeeping, communications, and warehousing services.

Personnel and employee-related services: Food, laundry, health, insurance, counseling, and vending machine services.

Source: Donald W. Dobler; Lamar Lee, Jr.; and David N. Burt. *Purchasing and Materials Management*, 4th ed. (New York: McGraw-Hill Book Company, 1984), p. 193.

The Standard Industrial Classification (SIC) Manual (1987) definition shown in Table 1-4 appears oriented toward U.S. Government economic data and record-keeping methods established many years ago. Although it contains most of the services an organization could possibly purchase, its classification process bears no relationship to the customer-buyer-supplier relationships known to exist in most organizations today.

The Federal Acquisition Regulation (FAR) (1992) definition reflected in Table 1-5 is very relevant to the public sector and to many private entities as well. One notable exception to this is R&D services. Most private firms refrain from contracting for this type of service in the interest of industrial security.

The Office of Federal Procurement Policy (OFPP) (1991) definition reflected in Table 1-6 is extremely broad in its coverage, but provides no classification or categorization system for services. For an adequate classification system the reader must look to one of the other references cited or, better still, develop a separate system.

TABLE 1-4   Services included in SIC Division I.

Includes establishments primarily engaged in providing a wide variety of services for individuals, business and government establishments, and other organizations.
Hotels and other lodging places
Establishments providing personal, business repair, and amusement services
Health, legal, engineering, and other professional services
Educational institutions
Membership organizations
Other miscellaneous services are included in this category.

Source: *Standard Industrial Classification Manual* (Washington, D.C.: Government Printing Office, 1987) p. 353.

TABLE 1-5   Service contracts as defined by the FAR.

Maintenance, overhaul, repair, servicing, rehabilitation, salvage, and modernization
Routine recurring maintenance of real property
Housekeeping and base services
Advisory and assistance services
Operation of government-owned equipment, facilities, and systems
Communications services
Architect–engineering (A&E)
Transportation and related services
Research and development (R&D).

Source: *Federal Acquisition Regulation (FAR)*. (Washington, D.C.: Government Printing Office, 1992), p. 37-1.

TABLE 1-6   Service contracts as defined in the Office of Federal Procurement Policy (OFPP) Proposed Policy Letter 92, Subject: Management Oversight of Service Contracting, dated December 20, 1991.

Services are identifiable tasks to be performed, rather than the delivery of an end item of supply. The term services also includes tasks that are delivered under a contract where the primary purpose of the contract is to provide supplies.

Source: *Federal Register.* (Washington, D.C.: Government Printing Office, 1991), p. 56 FR 66091.

In order to combine the best aspects of these different categories, the authors have developed six categories of services based on broad functional categories and service output. Both the private and public sectors are accommodated. The resulting categories include virtually all the service categories included in the six previous tables. Categories of purchased services used in this book are found in Table 1-7.

A quick scan of Table 1-7 will detect some overlap within the categories and undoubtedly suggest other appropriate descriptors. Some readers might object to the inclusion of certain types of personal service in the definition of *professional services.* This distinction is primarily important to the public sector, which has severe strictures against contracting for personal services. The reason for these strictures is that personal service contracts, either by their stated terms or by virtue of the manner in which they are administered, make the supplier personnel equivalent to buyer organization employees. Personal service contracts in both the public and private sectors obscure lines of authority and create internal friction when supplier personnel are paid differently from in-house personnel doing similar (or identical) work. As a general rule, public- and private-sector purchasing departments should resist awarding personal service contracts unless an urgent need exists and a capability to perform the work does not exist in-house. Personal service contracts should be initiated only after receipt of a valid requisition and, whenever possible, should be awarded on a price-competitive basis.

Still others may object to the categories of services this text will use on the grounds that they do not contain all types of services that might be purchased by an organization. This is true. Rather than listing *all* services, an attempt has been made to provide a framework for categorizing all services, regardless of their frequency of use.

Having achieved a workable, comprehensive categorization that can be used in a wide variety of organizations, let us turn to the contrast and comparison of supply purchasing with service purchasing. Both preaward (procurement) functions and postaward (administration) functions have been addressed.

TABLE 1-7   Categories of purchased services used in this book.

Facility-related services include: Real estate services; Architect-Engineering (A&E) and related services (that is, drafting, surveying, mapping, and soils investigation); construction; housekeeping services
(that is, janitorial, grounds maintenance, and guard services); real property (buildings and equipment) maintenance; operation of facilities, systems, and equipment; and utilities (other than telecommunications).

Materials/logistics services in support of operations include: Transportation services (inbound) and warehousing services (Production and MRO materials).

Materials/logistics services in support of marketing include: Transportation services (outbound); warehousing services (finished goods); R&D; and advertising.

Communication services include: Public relations services; photographic services; printing and publication services; telephone services; and ADP services.

Employee-support services include: Food, cafeteria, and vending machine services; health and dental insurance; travel support services; laundry services; and counselling services.

Professional services include: Engineering services (other than those provided by an architect–engineering firm); technical advisory services; expert consulting and advisory services; training and education services; medical services; dental services; legal services; auctioneering services; and mediation and arbitration services.

DIFFERENCES BETWEEN SUPPLY AND SERVICE PURCHASING

Individuals making the transition from supply and product purchasing to service purchasing are often struck first with the differences between the supply and service industries. The differences between supply and service purchasing are summarized in Table 1-8. These differences will be further explained in the text that follows Table 1-8.

Industry Characteristics

Many material and equipment suppliers have been obliged to invest substantial sums for plant and equipment before commencing operations, whereas some service suppliers can operate with little investment in facilities. Consequently, most service businesses are small (according to Small Business Administration standards). Many, in addition to being small, are small-disadvantaged (minority) or women-owned. Because of the large concentration of small and small-disadvantaged businesses among service providers, both public- and private-sector purchasing departments often try to further certain socioeconomic goals by setting service purchases aside exclusively for small or small-disadvantaged businesses. The combination of a heavy concentration of small and small-disadvantaged businesses with socioeconomic set-asides has caused most organizations to buy services from smaller, often less sophisticated, firms. Such purchases often present more problems for the buyer.

TABLE 1-8   Differences between supply and service purchasing.

Factor	Supply	Service
Industry	Stable with entry barriers	Few barriers to entry
Industry composition	Both large and small firms	Small and small-disadvantaged (Minority) firms dominate
Competition	Varies: Strong for private customers, often weak for public sector customers	Generally strong
Funding	Generally 100% "funded"	May be "funded" by fiscal year (particularly for public sector)
In-house competition	Formal make-or-buy decision making	Make-or-buy decision rules fuzzy or absent
Labor laws	Private—Fair Labor Standards Act (FLSA)	Private—Fair Labor Standards Act (FLSA) and Contract Work Hours and Safety Standards Act (CWHSSA)
	Public—FLSA and Walsh-Healey Public Contracts Act	Public—FLSA, CWHSSA, Service Contract Act (SCA), Davis-Bacon and "allied acts"
Description	Specification	Statement of work (other than construction), Specifications–drawings (construction)
In-house estimates	Detailed estimates less common	Detailed estimates absolutely necessary
Solicitation	Often oral	Generally written
Selection criteria	Often lowest price	Other factors as well as price often considered
Deliverables	Tangible personal property	Documents, studies, reports, completed projects and manyears
Ordering	Normally once	Often "as needed"
Bonding	Rare	Frequent
Inspection	Generally at "destination"	Generally at place of performance, (may be "destination")
Penalties for non-conformance	Normally rejection or return	Reperformance or reduced payment

TABLE 1-8   Differences between supply and service purchasing. (*continued*)

Factor	Supply	Service
Term of contract	Until final deliverable	Until project completion or on a multiple year basis
Extension options	Rarely used	Frequently used
Payment	Upon delivery	Upon project completion or monthly
Administration	Nominal	Extensive

The depth of competition present in service purchasing also surprises new buyers, particularly if they have come from a Government or public-sector supply purchasing background. Although many Government (particularly Department of Defense) supply purchases are sole source or limited source because of their specialized requirements, most service purchases are heavily competitive. The public sector has witnessed service purchases with as many as 20 or 30 offers, even for modestly sized contracts. One might question the economic efficiency of so many firms bidding on a job that only one can win. Receipt of two (or more) offers generally qualifies as "adequate price competition."

Funding Differences

Buyers new to public-sector (and sometimes private-sector) service purchasing may also be confounded by funding rules that differ from those to which they are accustomed. Supply purchases are almost always fully "funded." Service purchases, on the other hand, often span fiscal or calendar years. Federal government agencies, in particular, attempt to relate work effort closely to fiscal year funding and hence generally fund only the work needed in the current fiscal year. Public-sector service buyers and suppliers are normally very familiar with "Availability of Funds for the Next Fiscal Year" provisions, which tell service suppliers they will have contract work in the next fiscal year only if the necessary funds are appropriated.

In-House Competition

Another area of difference between service purchasing and supply purchasing is the make-or-buy decision. Both private- and public-sector organizations tend to have highly formalized make-or-buy decision-making procedures for supplies. This is often not the case for service purchases. Although the Federal Government has a very formal system for analyzing in-house versus contract services, the services for which it hires contractors are often incremental services it cannot perform in-house because of funding or personnel ceiling limits. Often most of a service function is performed in-house, with an incremental piece of the function performed by contract. Federal Government employees may be sitting side-by-side with contractor employees performing the same task. When one of the factions earns more than the other, conflict and ill-will result. In contrast, although some private-sector organizations have well-managed "outsourcing" programs, many organizations in this sector do not have a formal program for analyzing in-house versus contract service operations and often undertake contract operations irrespective of the comparative economies of the two alternatives.

Labor Law Issues

In the private sector, buyers have a limited number of labor laws to which they must adhere. In supply purchasing, buyers must adhere to the Fair Labor Standards Act (FLSA). In service purchasing, buyers must adhere to not only the Fair Labor Standards Act, but also the Contract Work Hours and Safety Standards Act (CWHSSA).

Federal-sector buyers of supplies must be familiar not only with the FLSA, but also with the Walsh-Healey Public Contracts Act. Prior to awarding a contract, federal-sector buyers must obtain Walsh-Healey certifications from suppliers confirming their status as manufacturers or regular dealers (and deal with protests from other firms who allege the low bidder fails to qualify under this criterion). Before and after awarding a contract, federal-sector buyers, under Walsh-Healey, must process suspension or debarment actions against vendors that have falsified their manufacturer or regular dealer status.

Federal-sector service buyers must adhere to the Service Contract Act (SCA) in addition to the CWHSSA (the latter act is designed primarily for construction-related work) and the FLSA. The SCA places a greater administrative burden on federal-sector buyers than does the Walsh-Healey act. Federal-sector service buyers cannot award a covered service contract until that contract contains a contract- and area-specific wage determination. The Department of Labor (DOL) in Washington, D.C. rarely issues such a determination before 90 days have elapsed from the date of initial request. After the contract is awarded federal-sector service buyers are held to strict SCA requirements for a new wage determination if they intend to extend the contract. In addition, the SCA limits the cost elements that can be adjusted on an extension to direct labor and related costs, which excludes material, overhead, general and administrative expense (G&A), or profit increases. The DOL requires federal-sector service buyers to help administer the law on their contracts and, if suspension or debarment action is warranted, initiate the action. A lengthy explanation of the impact of this law is available in Appendix A.

Federal-sector buyers of construction services have perhaps the greatest administrative burden of all because they must administer the Davis-Bacon Act and its related acts for DOL. A great number of pre- and postaward responsibilities and duties must be performed. A full discussion of these laws is beyond the scope of this chapter. A lengthy explanation of the impact of this law is available in Appendix B.

Descriptions of Requirements

Descriptions of requirements also differ in supply and service purchases. In supply purchases, items are often commercial or "off-the-shelf." The same specifications (with minor updates as necessary) can be used from purchase to purchase. Many supply buyers provide little, if any, input to the preparation of the typical supply specification. In service purchasing, the specifications (called statements of work) tend to be contract-specific. Moreover, statements of work generally require a technical/contracting *team approach*. Because they are contract-specific and developed under severe time constraints, statements of work are often less comprehensive and reflect less depth of understanding than supply specifications. This is particularly true where the organization has never performed the service and has never contracted for similar services before. Some organizations take the easy way out of this dilemma by asking the service supplier to write the statement of work. They do so, of course, at their own peril.

In-House Estimates

Although it is a good business practice to prepare detailed estimates for all purchases, service purchases demand the preparation of detailed in-house estimates. Service purchases are often awarded based on technical as well as cost considerations and after technical and cost negotiations. In many instances, buyers must rely on detailed in-house estimates (supplemented by an audit of records, if appropriate) in price negotiations. (Construction contracts likewise depend heavily on detailed estimates, not only as a basis for reviewing and verifying bid errors, but also as a means of establishing and verifying schedules of prices used in pricing contract changes and for making payments. This is a general industry practice that both private- and public-sector buyers are well advised to heed.)

Solicitation

Oral solicitations may suffice and are often used for off-the-shelf, highly standardized supplies. The highly individualized nature of services makes written solicitations necessary.

Contract Types

Service buyers must be adept in using various types of contracts, whereas supply buyers can often spend their entire career awarding firm-fixed-price (lump-sum or fixed-price line item) contracts or purchase orders. The indefiniteness of service requirements provides many circumstances where indefinite-quantity/indefinite-delivery, requirements, or time-and-material/labor-hour contract types are necessary and appropriate. Service contracts may require combination or composite contract types, with certain clearly defined contract services falling under a firm-fixed-price line item and other less clearly defined contract services falling under a requirements or time-and-materials line item(s). Applying firm-fixed-price contract type thinking to all service contracts is courting disaster that will manifest itself in problems with contract administration.

Supplier Selection Criteria

Unlike the majority of supply contracts, most service purchases (other than construction) will consider technical approach and experience to be at least as important as low price. Architect/engineering firms are, in fact, generally selected solely on technical qualifications; contracts are awarded based on negotiation of a fair and reasonable price with the best technically qualified firm. Other service purchases generally select the successful firm based on technical and cost proposal submittals, with lowest price being only one of the factors used in selection. Some organizations even assign price such a low weight that it has little effect on the selection decision. In the public sector, these purchases are considered negotiated procurements, and discussions will generally be held on both technical and price/cost matters.

Nature of Contract Deliverables

Unlike supply deliverables, which are usually of a tangible nature, service deliverables can take many forms. Good contracting for services would call for packaging services into discrete deliverable work units in order to avoid the appearance of personal service contracting. Unless the purchased service is measured in discrete work units, the buyer personnel administering the contract tend to deal with supplier personnel as if they were working directly for the buyer organization, thus creating the problems associated with personal service contracting.

Examples of discrete work packages include square feet of interior or external masonry wall painted, square meters or yards of lawn mowed, and numbers of guard posts manned. This type of work line item can be readily priced either as a lump-sum or a fixed-price line item. If unable to define requirements as discrete work packages, statements of work should detail time-and-material or labor-hour line items. The authors recommend using estimated man-hours for which labor rates (including base hourly rate, benefits, overhead, G & A, and profit) can be developed and applied. Total dollar estimates for materials (excluding labor, overhead, G & A, and profit) can be added to the total labor estimate to derive a total cost estimate for the work. Unlike discrete work package deliverables, which are usually amenable to measurement and review for quality, the output of time-and-material or labor-hour contracts is delivered in the form of man-hours. It is considerably more difficult to measure the quality of man-hours than it is to measure most discrete work items.

Ordering Differences

Supply purchasing (unless it is accomplished in a partnering, Manufacturing Resource Planning (MRP) or Just-in-Time (JIT) environment) generally involves a one-shot ordering process. Service purchasing, conversely, often necessitates using indefinite-quantity (blanket order) contracts, which rely heavily upon ordering "as needed." Most time-and-materials or labor-hour contracts are also of this nature. Although buyers generally attempt to develop lump-sum requirements, their ability to do so decreases as the complexity of the services, size of the contract, and the time period covered by the contract increases. Multiple ordering generally adds to the administrative work load, and an inability to develop lump-sum requirements leads either to complicated composite-type contracts or to multiple ordering.

Bonding Requirements

The frequency of bonding is another difference between supply and service purchasing. Although bonding is rarely required for supply purchases, construction contracts are almost always bonded. Bonding of nonconstruction service contracts represents an "in between" situation, with many buyers invoking bonding requirements on a business judgment basis.

Inspection Procedures

Inspection procedures also differ somewhat for supplies and services. Supplies of a noncritical nature are normally inspected at destination. Supplies of a critical nature will often warrant inspection at origin, before the items are shipped to the buyer's manufacturing facility. Services must always be inspected at the performance site (whether that be at destination or elsewhere). Suppliers that fail to deliver conforming items subject themselves to rejection or return of the items purchased. Service suppliers who fail to perform timely or acceptable quality service are all-too-often paid for their shoddy workmanship. This does not mean that service contracts cannot be written so as to assure adequate quality. It is the challenge of every statement of work writer to interject clear, unambiguous standards of quality and methodologies for measuring conformance. Contracts written with effective quality requirements enable the buyer to demand quality performance through either reperformance or reduction in payment for work not performed or performed below the requisite quality standard.

Penalties for Nonconformance

If supplies are substandard or do not meet the specifications, customers ordinarily reject the shipment, return it to the supplier, and refuse payment. It is possible for the supply buyer to agree to accept shipment in return for a price reduction, but ordinarily that is not done.

A service, once performed, cannot be returned to the manufacturer. If a service is substandard, the buyer will often insist on either reperformance or reduction in price, depending on the level of utility of the service as performed.

Terms of Performance

Term of Contract (Length), Use of Options.   Contract terms of performance often vary between supply and service purchases. One major difference is in the length of the contract term. Supply purchases generally terminate upon successful delivery or default in delivery. Service purchases will generally either terminate at project completion (sometimes years in the future), or be extended at the option of the buyer.

Although not uncommon in supply purchasing, renewal options are much more pervasive in service purchasing. Use of service contract renewal options facilitates annual schedule price adjustments based upon either economic price adjustment escalators/deescalators or prepriced line items. Although utility service contracts will often have a ten-year term, many organizations award service contracts for a base year, with several one-year options. The FLSA and SCA limit annual adjustments in labor and labor-related cost changes to SCA wage determinations for federal government service contracts.

Final Payment

Final payment for supply purchases is invariably made after receipt, inspection, and testing of merchandise and receipt of an acceptable invoice. Although final payment in construction contracts is made upon project completion and formal acceptance of the facility, service purchases generally call for monthly invoicing and payment through buyer choice (contract requirement). This is generally true whether the service is priced on a lump-sum or indefinite-quantity basis.

Amount of Contract Administration

The administration of service contracts is highly resource intensive. Service contracts are more likely to have a cost-reimbursement compensation structure than are supply contracts, which are invariably some type of fixed-price arrangement. Cost-reimbursement contracts require significantly more administration than fixed-price contracts. However, even fixed-price service contracts demand inspection and contract management surveillance at higher levels than are required for supply contracts. The combination of added labor law requirements, multiple provisions needed to implement various indefinite-quantity contract types, option pricing provisions, and detailed quality assurance/control requirements adds to service contract administration complexity.

Supply Versus Service Purchasing: Overall Effects of the Differences

One major result of the differences between supply and service purchasing is that the acquisition of services is much more paper-intensive. In addition to tailored statements of work, service purchases generally require written solicitations built around those statements of work. Tailored statements of work must be accompanied by tailored schedules and other terms and conditions. Service buyers rarely have the luxury (enjoyed by their supply buyer associates) of using time-saving oral solicitations to obtain quotations and proposals for their services. This administrative detail generally lengthens the lead time for service purchases. The procurement lead time for services is about two or three times longer than that for supply purchases. Advance purchasing plans for services should not disregard this difference.

Service purchasing is also more problem-laden than is supply purchasing. A comparison of the problems attendant to supply and service purchasing is shown in Table 1-9.

As should be apparent from the lists shown in Table 1-9, service purchasing is not only more complicated and paper-laden than most supply purchases, it also is more problem-prone. The added complications and paperwork are actually attempts to deal with and prevent some of the additional problems.

The next chapter provides the explanation of a process that can be used to advantage to facilitate the service contract solicitation and award process.

SUMMARY

To be most useful to purchasing practitioners, the word "service" should include definitions, categories, and classifications of services and the functions they support. Not all services are performed for all organizations, and some services are performed in the public sector only.

Professional services differ from personal services. The emphasis in professional service contracting is on the profession. Examples are law, medicine, engineering, and external auditing. The emphasis in personal service contracting, however, is more on the individual as a supplier of labor. Buying-organization managers directly supervise personal service workers. Personal service contracts cause dissention in the buying organization when personal service workers are paid differently from in-house employees doing the same job under the same supervision as noncontract employees.

The difficulties of service contracting can be decreased if the work can be

TABLE 1-9   Supply purchasing versus service purchasing: problems encountered.

Supply Purchasing	Service Purchasing
Late delivery	Nonperformance
Shortages/overages	
Nonconforming materials	Unsatisfactory performance
Specification too rigid	Statement of work too loose
	Organizational conflicts of interest
	Under- overabsorption of overhead
	Intellectual property or data rights conflicts
	Problems resulting from supplier working in buyer's facility
	Problems with continuity of operations if supplier defaults or is replaced by a successor

divided into discrete packages. If rational work packages cannot be developed, then the work cannot be described adequately for the statement of work, the contract must be based on time expended rather than on output, and quality is difficult to define and more difficult to determine on inspection.

Differences Between Supply Purchasing and Service Purchasing

1. Service businesses are generally less capital intensive; there is a high concentration of small and minority businesses and competition is fierce.
2. Service contracts often span several fiscal years.
3. Make-or-buy decision (in-house versus contract) rules tend to be fuzzy or nonexistent for services.
4. The administrative burden of labor laws is much greater for service contracts, particularly in the federal sector.
5. Drafting specifications (statements of work) for services is complicated and time-consuming because few services qualify as being off-the-shelf.
6. Preparation of in-house estimates for services is similarly complicated.
7. Solicitations for supply purchases are more likely to be oral than are service purchase solicitations.
8. The service buyer needs to be able to use a variety of contract types (including composite contracts).
9. Contracts for services are often awarded on the basis of technical merit at least as much as on price.
10. Service deliverables are generally not tangible property.
11. Service contracts are more likely to provide for purchases as-needed.
12. Bonding is much more common in service purchasing.
13. Inspecting supplies generally occurs at the destination; inspecting services occurs at the place of performance.
14. A service cannot be returned to the supplier; typical penalties for improper performance on service contracts are reperformance and reduced payment.
15. The service contract term is more likely to be extended with options.

The entire service purchasing process is more complex and paper-laden than is supply purchasing. The greater administrative burden lengthens the lead time needed to award service contracts.

2

The Advance Purchasing
Planning Process for Services

THE ADVANCE PURCHASING PLAN AS A
BASIS FOR SUPPLIER SELECTION

In service purchasing, as in supply purchasing, the key to developing sources capable of performing the organization's contract work is advance purchasing planning. Advance purchasing planning is the deliberate planning performed by personnel in the buying organization to coordinate and integrate the efforts required for a purchasing transaction.

Although the advance purchasing plan impacts on later steps in the service procurement process, selecting the right service supplier is pivotal to the objectives of the plan, which are timely and cost-effective procurement. Satisfying these objectives requires a combined, coordinated team effort from all personnel concerned, including the buyer, the buyer's technical representative, the engineering staff, and other affected parties. This advance planning process must address such issues as the following:

1. *Whether the service will be described in performance or design terms.*
2. *The target dates for beginning and completing the project.* A host of factors must be considered in setting such dates, including both performance and procurement lead times, fiscal year funding constraints, and the date (if any) by which the buying organization needs to have the services completed.
3. *The work cost estimate,* including the basis for that estimate, with supporting figures and documentation. Examples of estimate bases include: independent detailed cost estimate, project officer estimate, comparison of like effort, and level of effort.

4. *The deliverables that will be required* of the service supplier. If a completion-type contract is being used, the deliverables must be fully usable and identifiable. For a level-of-effort contract, the scope and duration of effort must be described. Many service contracts have deliverables expressed in man-months, man-weeks, or man-hours of effort.

5. *The list of known suppliers* that are considered potentially qualified and are interested in performing the work. To decide whether to set the purchase aside for certain socioeconomic classes, this list should indicate supplier size and status, that is, large, small, or small-disadvantaged (minority) business.

6. *The make-or-buy decision:* Whether formal consideration has been given to in-house performance of all or part of the work. This evaluation should address in-house capability and explain why performance of the required services in-house is inappropriate or uneconomical.

7. *The make-or-buy decision:* Whether formal consideration has been given to acquiring the required services from affiliated organizations. This issue is similar to the one in number 6, with the added consideration of whether the "interdivisional transfer" should be made at cost or with a profit attached.

8. *Small, small-disadvantaged business set-asides:* Whether the services are by nature appropriate for performance by small or small-disadvantaged (minority) businesses. If so, the the buyer must decide whether the depth of competition is great enough that the purchase can be set-aside exclusively for one of these business categories. Also, the buyer must decide whether to require the supplier to use small or small-disadvantaged business firms for subcontracting opportunities.

9. *Price competition:* The degree and extent of price competition to seek for the work. Possible efforts to promote competition include advertising in newspapers and trade publications, holding trade shows or "How to do business with our firm" seminars, providing draft solicitations or statements of work to the service-supplier community, dual sourcing, award on an "any-or-all" basis, using technical libraries, and so forth. Also, if this contract is likely to be followed by further purchases of a like or similar nature, a decision should be made on the efforts planned to allow or encourage competition for the later purchases. This could include things like second-source development, teaming arrangements, and so forth.

10. *For sole-source services:* If it appears that only one firm is capable of performing the work, a deliberate evaluation must be made of the major factors causing this situation.

11. *The major elements of risk* associated with the work must be identified. Three types of risk need to be evaluated:

- Technical,
- Schedule, and
- Cost.

Risk in each of these major areas should be identified as "high," "medium," or "low." The major risk drivers for medium- and high-risk items should be identified.

12. *Contract type:* Given the nature of the product or service and the level of risk, a deliberate effort must be made to select the appropriate contract type. The advance purchasing planning team should be able to explain why it preferred the chosen contract type.

13. *Procurement method:* Given all of these decisions, the team must determine the appropriate procurement method to be used (for example, competitive bidding, technical competition followed by sole-source negotiations, or selection based on technical and management factors in addition to price/cost). Although consultants and other professional service suppliers are often selected based on a combination of technical and price factors, competitive bidding should be considered an option in every service purchase. If factors other than price are used to make the selection, the advance planning team should develop a source-selection plan and solicitation evaluation criteria for the buyer and the evaluation team.

14. *Special considerations:* The advance planning team will need to address other special considerations that may impact the service procurement. For example, the procurement may involve special environmental considerations or environmental impact statements (EIS/EA) (often required for certain facilities type services). Specific client/user approval may be required for multiple year contracting (a contract term of three years or more), options, economic price adjustment provisions, and so forth.

15. *Schedule requirements:* The advance planning team will need to address schedule requirements. The product of this effort should be a milestone schedule, agreed to by all members of the team, for at least the following milestones.

	Month/Year
Requisition to purchasing	_____
Statement of work to purchasing	_____
Solicitation issued	_____
Offers received	_____
Source selection/negotiation complete	_____
Contract award	_____
Authority to proceed	_____

16. *Temporary personal service contracts*: Buyers will want their organizations' advance purchasing planning teams to consider whether the services to be acquired could be performed on a temporary contract basis (as opposed to a temporary direct-hire basis). Temporary service contracts are generally considered contracts for personal services because the workers provided under these contracts are supervised by the buyers' firms and are treated as in-house employees but are paid by their employing agency. (These agencies mark up their salaries with overhead and profit.)

A synopsis of the issues addressed in the advance purchasing plan is presented in Table 2-1.

If the advance purchasing plan has been completely, thoughtfully, carefully prepared, identifying and selecting a good service supplier becomes much easier. The right supplier responds to the solicitation with the best evidence of willingness and ability to perform the work as described in the advance plan, on the desired schedule (including start date, end date, and milestones), under the desired contract type, for the best price.

Possible sources of service supply (as indicated in 5,6,7,8, and 14 in the advance planning process list) include external suppliers (possibly small-disadvantaged businesses), in-house personnel, personnel from other divisions

TABLE 2-1   Issues addressed in the advance purchasing plan.

Service description: Performance terms versus design terms.

Target dates: Dates for beginning and completing the project.

The cost estimate, the basis for that estimate, supporting figures and documentation.

The deliverables that will be required of the service supplier.

The list of known suppliers possibly qualified and interested in performing the work.

Make-or-buy: Whether formal consideration has been given to performance either in-house or by affiliated organizations.

Small or small-disadvantaged (minority) business: Whether the services are appropriate for performance by such firms.

Price competition: The degree and extent to seek.

For sole-source services: A deliberate evaluation must be made of the major factors creating this situation.

Major elements of technical, schedule, and cost risk.

Selection of the appropriate contract type.

Selection of procurement method: Competitive bidding, technical competition followed by sole-source negotiations, or choice based on technical/management factors as well as price/cost.

Schedule requirements and performance milestones.

Could the services be performed on a temporary contract basis?

Other considerations that may impact the service procurement.

---

of the buying organization, and temporary service workers. Contracting with temporary service workers is possibly the most difficult.

GUIDELINES FOR TEMPORARY SERVICE CONTRACTING

Under normal circumstances, temporary personal services should be purchased under competitively negotiated agreements. Such agreements (normally blanket purchase agreements) should generally be negotiated annually, but may be done on a one-time purchase order basis, particularly for urgent requirements not covered by an agreement.

If an agreement with an individual is necessary, a statement should be received from that individual indicating that he or she is self-employed and has an IRS self-employed identification number and a certificate of liability insurance.

No temporary personal services personnel should be employed without a valid contract or order under an existing contract. Personal service contracts should be executed by the organization's Purchasing Department and should contain the items listed in Table 2-2.

Billings on blanket purchase agreements/contracts negotiated for temporary personal services should be initiated by an invoice from the supplier. The supplier should be responsible for having its employees complete a time card and having the requesting department approve time cards covered by the contract. The buying organization's Accounts Payable Department should match time cards submitted by the requesting department with the service invoice.

The buyer should provide a monthly report of all temporary personal service agreements to Purchasing management. Table 2-3 lists the data that should be included in the reports.

The next chapter will cover guidance on development of the service contract statement of work.

TABLE 2-2   Items belonging in personal service contracts.

An all-inclusive labor-hour rate for each type of personnel;
Formulas for developing hourly rates for billing both straight time and overtime wages;
Instructions for invoicing;
Funding limitations;
Delineation of responsibility for handling proprietary information;
Workman's compensation and insurance requirements;
Record-keeping responsibilities; and
Duration of assignment.

TABLE 2-3   Data belonging in reports of personal service contracts.

Purchased personal service agreement identification number;
Name of firm or individual providing the service;
Identification of the originator;
Description of service being provided;
Authorized value of the agreement; and
Period of time covered by the agreement.

SUMMARY

The Advance Purchasing Plan as a Basis for Supplier Selection

A comprehensive advance purchasing plan is necessary for timely and cost-effective procurement. The supplier selection process is the focal point of the plan. If the issues involved in the advance purchasing plan have been properly identified and analyzed, identifying and selecting the right service supplier becomes much easier. The supplier selected should respond to the solicitation in a manner that demonstrates the greatest ability to perform the work as described in the advance plan, on the desired schedule (including start date, end date, and milestones), under the desired contract type, for the best value (often lowest price).

Issues Addressed in the Advanced Purchasing Plan

1. Should the service description be phrased in performance or design terms?
2. What should be the target dates for beginning and completing the project?
3. What is the estimated cost for the work? On what is that estimate based? What supporting figures and documentation exist?
4. What deliverables should be required of the service supplier?
5. What individuals and/or organizations should be included on a list of known suppliers possibly qualified and/or interested in performing the work?
6. Has formal consideration been given to performing the work either in-house or through affiliated organizations? If not, should such participation be considered?
7. Are the services appropriate for performance by small or small-disadvantaged (minority) business firms? If so, should the services be set-aside for such firms?

8. What degree of price competition should the firm seek, and what level of effort should be expended to seek it?
9. Is the service available from only one source? If so, what are the major factors creating this situation?
10. What are the major elements of technical, schedule, and cost risk?
11. What contract type would be appropriate for this purchase?
12. Which procurement method (competitive bidding, technical competition followed by sole-source negotiations, or choice based on technical/management factors as well as price/cost) would be most appropriate for this purchase?
13. What should be the schedule requirements and performance milestones?
14. Could the services be performed on a temporary contract basis?
15. What other considerations could impact the service procurement?

134453

3

The Service Contract Statement of Work

The service contract statement of work establishes and defines all requirements for supplier effort. The level of detail employed in writing the statement of work is important. If the work description is not sufficiently definitive, some service suppliers may not propose because they are either uncertain about the risks involved or because they fail to recognize their own capability to perform the work. On the other hand, if the statement of work is too restrictive, competent service suppliers may refuse to respond because they feel that their creative, alternate approaches will not be permitted.

The service statement of work should have, as a minimum, four major sections, including those identified in Table 3-1.

A brief explanation of each section follows.

GENERAL SCOPE OF WORK

This section should include background and introductory information for the procurement. The overall objectives of the work effort should be identified. A "work or services excluded" provision may be used here, but should be used with extreme care to avoid implying that any work not specifically excluded is automatically included. A work or services excluded provision

TABLE 3-1   Major sections of the service work statement.

General scope of the work
Documents and references applicable to the work.
Explicit requirements for work performance.
Progress reports to be submitted during the life of the contract.

may be useful to clarify the scope of complicated multifunction contracts, especially if some of the work has already been performed.

DOCUMENTS AND REFERENCES

The documents and references that will be invoked in the explicit requirements section of the statement of work should be listed by document number and title. documents may include standards, specifications, and other references needed to identify and clarify specific work tasks and deliverable products. Documents listed in this section should be limited to those meeting the minimal needs identified in the explicit requirements section of the statement of work. A list of definitions may be included if necessary. Normally the definitions themselves should all appear in one place. Although the preferred place is in the body of the solicitation, a "definitions—technical" provision can be placed in this section to facilitate reading the technical section.

EXPLICIT REQUIREMENTS

The explicit requirements section must address comprehensive technical specifications describing the services required, how often they are required, performance indicators and required standards, and other information needed by the service supplier to perform the contract's technical requirements. This section should also specify buyer-furnished property and services (if any) as distinct from supplier-furnished property and services.

PROGRESS REPORTS

This section should contain a description of the status reports that will be used to monitor contract progress. For some service contracts, status reports or study results may be the only tangible deliverable.

Writing a statement of work to make it "contractible" and "administrable" is a serious challenge. Preparation of the statement of work, like that of most other documents in the purchasing process, requires careful planning. This planning encompasses the steps listed in Table 3-2.

After the plan has been completed, the team selected to write the statement of work should approach its development in a systematic manner. The steps that should generally be included in the preparation process are shown in Table 3-3.

Preparing the statement of work demands a total team effort. If the team contains several technical persons with each assigned to a different section

TABLE 3-2   **Major steps in the service work statement planning process.**

Review the requirements and documents authorizing the program or project for which the service or work will be needed.

Review the various policy documents related to the type of procurement being considered. This effort results in a bibliography citing all the policy documents that will be needed by the team preparing the statement of work.

Identify potential cost drivers. Only necessary cost drivers should be included in the statement of work, and they should be scaled to the minimal needs of the project.

Establish a preliminary work breakdown structure. This helps divide the work into its component parts. Service contract work breakdown structures are usually simple enough that they need not go beyond three levels of work.

Identify the organizations and individuals that should help prepare work statements and determine their roles and responsibilities. Creating the proper team is critical to generate an effective statement of work.

Describe work tasks in terms of the data that will be needed. So-called "work words" (a representative list is attached as Appendix C) must be used for this purpose.

Specify service tasks in performance terms where feasible. The team must specify *what* is to be done rather than *how*. Review all referenced documents to avoid including unnecessary requirements.

Prepare a detailed list of items needed in the work statement to aid in making assignments to team members.

TABLE 3-3   **Major steps in service work statement preparation.**

Divide the work into logical component parts.

Define the order in which the work tasks will be covered.

Identify those components of the required tasks that have already been defined in existing specifications, standards, or practices. The team must then assure that the appropriate reference documents are listed in the "documents and references" section and invoked in the explicit requirements section of the statement of work.

Isolate those tasks that will require additional research.

Identify those functions or aspects of the work that will require special care in presentation within the statement of work.

Determine the areas where additional help will be required and seek out the needed assistance in a timely fashion.

or task area, a technical team leader must be appointed to assure close coordination and integration of all the technical writing efforts.

The buyer must be available at all times both as a participating writer and as an advisor. Continuous discussion between the technical and buyer components of the preparation team is necessary to ensure that the statement of work will be consistent with the contract type to be employed as well as the schedule(s) of prices and services. A statement of work written around a firm-fixed-price contract assumption will not match an indefinite-delivery type or time-and-materials schedule. Conventionally prepared statements of work (those prepared without the use of a team approach) will often contain such discrepancies.

Care should be taken to state requirements very clearly. Failure to communicate requirements prevents both buyer and supplier from listing necessary resources, thus thwarting accurate cost estimating. It also prevents the technical representative from determining whether the supplier has complied with requirements, and therefore from signing the acceptance report.

Clarity can be improved in several ways when writing a work statement. One way is to avoid using passive verbs. Another is to craft the headings and subsections carefully. Headings should be grammatically correct, consistent with text and subheadings, and numbered using some standard system. General information should be separated from guidance and direction. Carefully distinguish between workdays and calendar days to improve clarity when specifying time frames for start and delivery dates.

In writing requirements, it is easy to focus on describing the work and slight descriptions of quality assurance. Quality assurance requirements should be considered for the total life of the requirements. When a contract covers both hardware and software, quality assurance requirements should be included for both.

In writing the work statement, the preparation team should use work words (preferably in the active tense), avoid inherently ambiguous terms and grammar, and avoid requirements that need agreement at some future date after contract award. A list of ambiguous terms is attached as Appendix D. A sample statement of work that uses work words and avoids ambiguity is attached as Appendix E.

Common errors found in statements of work are summarized in Table 3-4.

SUMMARY

The service contract statement of work defines what the service supplier is supposed to do. It must be sufficiently definitive without being too restrictive. It should include the following major sections:

1. Scope of the work—background and introductory information, including major objectives of the work.
2. Documents and references applicable to the work—a list of all documents that will be referenced.
3. Explicit requirements for work performance—comprehensive technical specifications for the work.
4. Progress reports—descriptions of the status reports the supplier will be expected to submit during the life of the contract.

TABLE 3-4   Errors commonly found in work statements.

Requirements are overstated (gold-plated) or biased in favor of one source.

Specific duties and tasks required of the service supplier are unclearly stated.

Relevant reference documents are either omitted or improperly cited; nonpertinent reference documents are cited.

Quality assurance requirements are absent or incomplete.

General information, guidance and direction are mixed together.

Some line item deliverable dates have been omitted.

References to elapsed time do not distinguish between calendar and workdays.

Headings contain errors, are incompatible with subheadings or text, or are not numbered properly.

Cross-references to provisions and extraneous materials remain.

Required reports and data items are not compatible with task requirements or are otherwise extraneous and irrelevant.

Buyer obligations to the supplier (buyer-furnished materials and services) are not clearly described.

Loopholes permitting undesirable performance methods remain.

Catch-all statements have not been eliminated.

Work breakdown structure has been omitted.

Control points and milestones are not stated.

Reports and documentation unnecessary for control, documenting results, or follow-on procurement are nonetheless required.

Preparing an adequate statement of work requires planning. The planning process should include reviewing the requirements and company policy toward the contemplated procurement type, preparing a work breakdown schedule, preparing a list of persons who should be involved in formal drafting of the statement of work, and reviewing documents to discover if any parts of the work already have a written specification.

The buyer should lead the team that drafts the statement of work, although the team will usually include a technical group with its own appointed group leader. Care must be taken to avoid inconsistencies, inaccuracies, biases, lack of clarity, omissions of relevant information and spelling/grammatical errors.

4

Contract Types Appropriate for Services

A well-written contract must describe or specify the items listed in Table 4-1 in sufficient detail.

Although the items in Table 4-1 must be included in some form or another in all contracts, they take unique forms in service contracts. Some of these

TABLE 4-1   Items specified in a well-written service contract.

The work to be performed.

The service price(s).

The quantity of services ordered. If the quantity is not firm, the procedures for ordering services under the contract should be stated.

The details for performance of the services, including where and when the services will be performed.

The term or length of the agreement.

Terms and conditions (provisions) that provide procedures for:

Allocating risk.

Payment.

Funding, particularly if the contract spans multiple fiscal years for the buying organization or is incrementally funded.

Inspection and acceptance of the services and actions the buyer can take if performance is unsatisfactory.

Making changes to the contract.

Extending the term of the agreement.

Buyer audit of records.

Socioeconomic issues—small and minority business preferences and set-asides, environmental requirements, and so forth.

Buyer termination of the contract for his or her organization's convenience or supplier default.

Handling disputes and disagreements.

An agreed-upon legal forum and law should litigation become necessary.

unique forms are covered in the next chapter. The automated contract preparation systems that many organizations now have can help ensure that these items have been included in their contracts.

A good contract (service or otherwise) must accomplish the following:

1. Allocate risk between the buyer and supplier,
2. Provide for an appropriate method of ordering work, and
3. Provide for an appropriate payment scheme.

Different procurement situations warrant different approaches to risk allocation, ordering and payment. Creating different compensation arrangements to fit different situations has resulted in a variety of contract types.

One of the most challenging tasks for the service buyer is to coordinate (and correlate) all the different elements that must be included in a typical service contract. Two elements that must correlate are the statement of work (previous chapter) and the compensation arrangement and/or contract type (this chapter). Service contracts that fail to achieve their performance objectives often do so because the statement of work is inconsistent with the risk allocation, and ordering and payment terms implicit in the contract type. In a service purchase the person preparing the statement of work (an engineer or other technical type) must work closely with the person structuring the contract (the buyer in most cases). Preparing the statement of work and structuring the contract type must be accomplished on a team basis, preferably during the advance planning process discussed in chapter 2.

Selecting the contract type is complicated by the interacting facts that the choice must be made before the contract is signed and that the contract should be signed before performance. This can result in selecting a compensation structure before the parties have adequate information on which to base their decision.

Things to consider when selecting a compensation arrangement (and therefore the contract type) are identified in Table 4-2.

The procurement conditions listed in Table 4-2 will be referred to repeatedly in the following chapter.

General rules to keep in mind during the following discussion of contract types are listed in Table 4-3.

Proper risk assessment is critical in selecting the contract type that presents the supplier with the greatest incentive for efficient and economical performance. For complex procurements, buyers should get project office technical support and jointly prepare input for the buyer's management.

TABLE 4-2   Considerations when selecting a contract type.

The levels and types of risk the service supplier is willing to bear.
The type and amount of work: Can it be accurately defined before the contract is signed?
Whether the supplier is a profit or a nonprofit organization.
Whether the supplier would be motivated to greater performance by using incentive payments.
Criteria for determining the size of any incentive payments: Are they subjective or objective?
Complexity of the method of determining ordering and payment: Do the benefits of more complex methods outweigh the costs?

CONTRACT TYPES

Fixed-Price Family

Firm-Fixed-Price

A firm-fixed-price contract provides a price that is not subject to any adjustment on the basis of the supplier's actual costs in performing the contract. This contract type places full risk and responsibility for all costs and resulting profit or loss on the supplier. It provides maximum incentive for the supplier to control costs and perform effectively. The buyer's administrative burden is minimal.

A firm-fixed-price contract is suitable for acquiring services if the buyer has reasonably definitive work statements and when fair and reasonable prices can be established at the outset.

Fixed-Price With Economic Price Adjustment
or Escalation

A fixed-price contract with economic price adjustment provides for upward and downward revision of the stated contract price upon the occurrence of specified contingencies. Economic price adjustments are generally based on one of three things:

1. *Established prices*: Changes in supplier payment are based on increases or decreases from an agreed-upon price level found in published or other-

---

TABLE 4-3   General rules of contract type selection.

Firm-fixed-price, indefinite-delivery (blanket order) type, and time-and-materials and labor-hour (or a combination of these) are most common in service contracting, although cost reimbursement and incentive contracts may also be used.
The cost-plus-percentage-of-cost contract should not be used.
A firm-fixed-price contract should be used whenever practical; when a firm-fixed-price is not used, the buyer should state the reason(s) why in the negotiation memorandum.

---

wise established prices of either the contract end-items or of some other specified item(s).
2. *Actual costs of labor or material*: Changes in supplier payment are based on increases or decreases in specified costs of labor or material that the supplier actually experiences during contract performance.
3. *Cost indexes of labor or material*: Supplier payment adjustments are based on increases or decreases in labor or material cost standards or indexes that are specifically identified in the contract.

A fixed-price contract with economic price adjustment may be used when:

1. There is serious doubt that market or labor conditions will remain stable during an extended period of contract performance; and
2. Contingencies that would otherwise be included in the contract price can be identified and covered separately in the contract.

Price adjustments based on established prices should normally be restricted to industrywide contingencies. Price adjustments based on labor and material costs should be limited to contingencies beyond the supplier's control.

A fixed-price contract with economic price adjustment should not be used unless it is necessary either to protect against significant fluctuations in the supplier's labor or material costs or to provide for contract price adjustment in the event of changes in the supplier's established prices.

Fixed-Price Incentive

A fixed-price incentive contract is a fixed-price instrument that establishes the final contract price, adjusting the supplier's profit in the process, using a formula based on accrued costs and performance factors. The final price is subject to a price ceiling negotiated at the outset.

A fixed-price incentive contract is appropriate when the following occur:

1. A firm-fixed-price contract is not suitable because of uncertainties over long-term market conditions;
2. Circumstances of the purchase, including the nature of the supplies or services being acquired, are such that requiring the supplier to assume a degree of cost responsibility will provide a positive profit incentive for effective cost control and performance; and
3. In the case of a contract with incentives for technical performance and/or delivery, the performance requirements provide a reasonable opportunity for the incentives to have a meaningful impact on the supplier's management of the work.

A fixed-price incentive contract should be used only when the following occur:

1. It is likely to be less costly than any other contract type;
2. Obtaining supplies or services of the kind or quality required is impractical without using this type of contract (for example, the supplier of a one-of-a-kind item resists other contract types);
3. The supplier's accounting system is capable of providing data for negotiating the final cost and incentive price revision formula at the beginning of the contract time frame; and
4. Adequate cost information for establishing reasonably firm targets is available at the time the contract is initially negotiated.

Indefinite-Delivery (Blanket Order) Type

Indefinite-delivery (blanket order) type contracts are sometimes called "open-end" or "term" contracts. They are quite frequently employed in service contracts, either in pure form or in combination with other types such as firm-fixed-price and time-and-materials or labor-hour. There are three basic forms of indefinite-delivery (blanket order) type contracts: requirements contracts, indefinite-quantity/indefinite-delivery, and definite-quantity/indefinite-delivery. Since the first two are more commonly used in service contracting than the third, this text will explore them in detail.

Indefinite-Quantity/Indefinite-Delivery (IQID)
Contracts

The IQID contract establishes firm-fixed unit prices for the units of work sought by the buyer. It states a guaranteed minimum quantity (base amount) and an estimated maximum quantity (ceiling or cap). This contract type is used when the buyer is seeking a service that requires high mobilization or start-up costs that would not be recoverable unless a minimum percentage of the total estimated services were actually ordered. The base amount should be more than just a nominal quantity, but should not exceed the total amount the buyer feels certain will be needed. This base provides the service supplier with a minimum upon which to offer and a means to recover the costs of mobilization or start-up.

IQID contracts provide the buyer with certain benefits. If the supplier's performance is poor, the supplier may be paid for the guaranteed minimum and the contract closed. A new solicitation and subsequent contract for the service can then be issued. The buyer should be aware, however, that in a new solicitation, there is no guarantee that the same supplier will not be the lowest offeror.

When an IQID contract is awarded, the buyer is generally authorized to order any number of units up to the maximum amount estimated for each work item in the schedule. The supplier is then responsible for supplying the minimum quantities and additional quantities up to that maximum. If the buyer fails to order the base amount, the supplier must still be paid the minimum amount guaranteed by the contract.

Funds for this type of contract are obligated only for the guaranteed base amount. The funds for units of work in excess of the base are obligated through delivery orders as the items or services are procured by the buyer.

Indefinite-Quantity/Indefinite-Delivery Example:
On-Call Vehicle Maintenance
Situation: Using historical data from maintenance records, the buyer determines that between 200 and 300 vehicles will require repair during the year. The number of repairs varies based on the amount of work each vehicle performs.

The buyer knows:

a. The estimated amount of work based on historical data;
b. The nature of the work (that is, vehicle maintenance); and
c. Sound cost estimates for different types of maintenance can be established prior to contracting.

The buyer does not know:

a. When the work will be required during the year;
b. What specific types of maintenance will be required; and
c. What the exact number of maintenance visits will be.

Appropriate contract type: Indefinite-quantity/indefinite-delivery
Why: It is possible to establish unit prices that are fixed and not subject to change. However, neither the quantity nor the frequency of work is definite. As a variety of maintenance types is involved, it would be in the buyer's best interest to obtain a separate price for each type of maintenance.

An IQID contract will provide the buyer with a means of guaranteeing to the supplier that the mobilization costs and some portion of the equipment costs could be realized whether the need actually equaled the estimate. The contract will also provide the buyer with a means of ordering the service on an as-needed basis. The buyer should contact the facilities manager and obtain a more specific breakdown of the types of maintenance service along with a historical estimate of the quantities involved. This will enable the offeror to have some insight into the amount of additional equipment required (if any). The risk to the buyer associated with this type contract is greater than that under a firm-fixed price contract because of the need to issue delivery orders for all work exceeding the guaranteed quantity.

Requirements Contracts

Requirements contracts also establish firm-fixed unit prices. Quantities stated in the schedule are estimated, not purchased by the contract award. The stated quantities are used only for evaluating offers and determining the low offeror. Offerors are put on notice that some, all, or none (heaven forbid!) of the work may be ordered. The contract guarantees that, during the term of the contract, any contract work of the types listed in the schedule will be procured from this supplier. This guarantee precludes performance of such work by the buyer organization's in-house forces unless the contract contains a provision that, under specified circumstances, the buyer reserves the right to use in-house employees. Such reservations must be very explicit.

The solicitation package for a requirements contract must clearly state that estimated quantities shown are solely for offering and offer evaluation purposes. The solicitation documents include a reasonable overall ordering ceiling or cap and limits on both the amount of any single delivery order and the number of delivery orders that may be placed at any one time under the contract. This ceiling protects the supplier from being inundated by an unanticipated work load and allows the buyer to solicit for large jobs separately.

The requirements contract does not obligate funds at the time the contract is awarded. Funds are obligated when delivery orders are issued pursuant to terms of the contract, which does not occur until after the item or service in question is required.

Because none of the work is guaranteed, the requirements contract does not provide the supplier any insight into how to gear up for the work. It provides only an estimate on which to base minimum levels of personnel, supplies, and equipment. Due to the unknowns associated with this type of contracting, its use may attract few offerors.

Requirements Contract Example: Grass Cutting

Situation: The buyer is required to maintain 100 acres of grassed area. Historical data indicates that in some years there may be extended periods of time in which no rain falls during the growing season. It is estimated that during a normal year the grass must be cut at least 28 times, but experience shows dry years in which it needed to be cut only 14 times. The frequency of the cuts depends on the rainfall. Three days of heavy rain and a day of sunshine makes the grass grow so rapidly it may require cutting on the fifth day rather than on the seventh day. If a dry spell follows, the grass may not need to be cut for ten or more days. The buyer would like to order the cuttings only when they are needed.

The buyer knows:

a. What the task is: grass cutting is easily definable;
b. That 100 acres require the service (note that the frequency of the cuts is the variable in this problem—not the acres to be cut);
c. A reasonable estimate of the number of cuts to be required; and
d. That a sound estimate of the cost per cut can be established prior to contracting.

The buyer does not know:

a. The actual number of cuts that will be required; and
b. At what intervals the work will be required.

Appropriate contract type: Requirements contract

Why: It is possible to establish a fixed unit price that is not subject to change. Under the terms of the contract the actual amount of work is fully controlled by the buyer. No obligation of funds occurs until a delivery order is issued.

The risk to the buyer is greater under this contract type than under a firm-fixed unit price contract because of the need to issue delivery orders for all work.

Indefinite-Delivery (Blanket Order) Ordering Issues

When using indefinite-delivery (blanket order) type contracts the following definitions must be clearly understood:

Definitions

Minimum Order   The minimum quantity on any one delivery order/authorization. The minimum should be set high enough to make accomplishment economically feasible for the supplier.

Maximum Order   The maximum amount that can be ordered at any one time. This limitation should be set at a level that will prevent the supplier from becoming so inundated with work that he or she will be unable to perform efficiently.

Minimum (Base) Guarantee   A guaranteed quantity or dollar value, applicable only to indefinite-quantity/indefinite-delivery type contracts, that establishes the minimum obligation to the supplier. The buying organization must pay for the minimum even if the total of all delivery orders or authorizations does not equal that amount. *Do not confuse this with minimum order.*

Maximum Contract Value   This is a ceiling or cap on the total amount the buyer can order from the supplier under the contract, and should be included in both IQID and requirements contracts. This cap may be stated in dollars or quantity percentages and should normally be in the realm of 200 percent over the estimated quantities being used as the basis for establishing the low offeror.

In indefinite-delivery (blanket order) type contracts, the demand for the items or service is based on *need* rather than on a *pre–arranged* schedule of delivery. Consequently, the buyer must issue a delivery order every time he or she wants the supplier to provide any of the services (or goods) ordered under the contract. Both the solicitation package and the contract document should specify how the scheduled items/work are to be ordered. Once the guaranteed minimum (if there is one) has been reached, the delivery order serves not only to state the quantities of the work units to be delivered, but also to establish a financial obligation on the buyer's part. For this reason delivery orders must be supported by a financial document (requisition) at the time of issue. To complete the obligation/payment cycle, a copy of each delivery order will usually accompany the invoice when it is submitted to Accounting to initiate payment.

Two basic methods of ordering are available to the buyer:

1. *Order for services:* Most purchase order forms provide the buyer with a means of furnishing the supplier with all the information related to the items/work being ordered, including accounting data chargeable.
2. *Letter format:* The letter format must include the items listed in Table 4-4:

Since the buying organization will not want to pay for work before it is accomplished, the need to commit funds at issuance of the delivery order creates a problem. To prevent internal audit complaints, one needs to begin issuing dual delivery orders at the onset of contract administration. The first

TABLE 4-4   Elements of a letter format delivery order.

Specific statements (descriptions) of work to be ordered.
Quantities.
Value of each line item of work and an overall total.
Dates for starting and completing the work.
Complete accounting data as chargeable to the various "cost codes" for the work authorized.
The contract number.
A delivery order number in consecutive sequence for each delivery order associated with the contract.

delivery order can be issued at the beginning of the contract, before work is begun. It should set forth a dollar amount (about ½ of estimated contract price or the amount then available if less than the estimated contract price) and state "for work to be authorized" during the month of _____ _____ (fill in coming month as appropriate). After work is authorized (keep a record so the amount of delivery order 1 is not exceeded), completed, and accepted for that month and payment can be made, delivery order 1 (modified) should be issued. The modified delivery order should itemize the specific work to be paid for, set forth the quantities, unit prices and totals therefor, and ultimately increase or decrease the amount of money established by delivery order 1.

Estimating Work Units Under Indefinite-Delivery Type Contracts

Indefinite-delivery (blanket order) type contracts require an estimate of the probable number of work units the buyer will procure during the contract period. The buyer makes the estimate based on available historical data and on funding constraints associated with the project.

The importance of basing this estimate on historical data cannot be overemphasized. Inaccurate estimates increase the risk for the buyer. This occurs because the supplier needs to build into the unit price costs associated with the delivery of the item(s) or service plus a reasonable profit margin. Some of those costs, including costs for mobilization and equipment, are constant regardless of the number of units required. Overestimates of the quantity result in low unit prices and underestimates result in high unit prices. If the buyer exceeds the estimate, the excess work will cost the buyer more than it would have if the estimate had been more accurate. Conversely, when the buyer does not call for the units estimated, the supplier suffers losses because mobilization costs, equipment costs, and profit cannot be recovered. The result is a disgruntled supplier and a potential claim against the buyer. A wise buyer does not cause a service supplier hardships.

Comparing Indefinite-Delivery (Blanket Order) Type Contracts

Table 4-5 compares IQID and requirements contracts with respect to their essential elements, limitations, and suitability.

Cost-Reimbursement Family

Cost-reimbursement types of contracts are suitable for use only when uncertainties involved in contract performance do not permit costs to be estimated with sufficient accuracy to use any type of fixed-price contract.

TABLE 4-5   Types of contracts: comparison and summary.

Indefinite-Quantity/Indefinite-Delivery

Essential elements:

A target amount of each item is included for offer evaluation purposes.

A stated minimum (guarantee) to be ordered by the buyer during the contract period. The minimum guarantee must be more than a nominal quantity (reasonable), yet it should not exceed the amount the buyer is fairly certain to order.

A maximum total amount to be ordered should be specified.

Method of ordering work must be stated.

Minimum and maximum orders allowable under the contract must be specified.

Limitations:

Funds are obligated by minimum (guaranteed) amount and thereafter by individual orders.

Provides flexible quantity and delivery schedule with limited buyer obligation.

A fixed unit price schedule (schedule of prices), which provides pricing basis for items to be ordered, is required prior to award.

Suitability:

Primarily suited for work that will be needed during a specific contract period when the exact time and quantity is unknown, although the buyer can guarantee that total orders will fall within a given range defined by specific maximum and minimum total quantities.

Requirements

Essential elements:

A maximum total amount to be ordered should be specified.

Method of ordering work must be stated.

Minimum/maximum orders allowable under the contract must be specified.

An agreement to order only from the contracting supplier any of the types of supplies and services described in the contract as long as the contract is in force.

Estimated total quantities replace total maxima and minima, and are used for offer evaluation.

A clear statement there is no guaranteed minimum (obligation is solely based on need required to be filled by that supplier).

Limitations:

Funds are obligated by each order and not by contract.

Provides flexibility in quantity and delivery schedule as orders are placed only after need materializes.

Suitability:

Primarily suited for work that will be needed during a specific contract period when the exact time and quantity is unknown.

A cost-reimbursement contract should be used only under the following circumstances:

1. The supplier's accounting system is adequate for determining costs applicable to the contract;
2. Appropriate surveillance during performance will provide reasonable assurance that efficient methods and effective cost controls are used; and
3. This contract type is likely to be less costly than any other type or it is impractical to obtain supplies or services of the kind or quality required without the use of this contract type.

Cost No-Fee and Cost Sharing

Cost contracts with no fee and cost sharing contracts are both cost-reimbursement contracts in which the supplier receives no fee. These cost contracts may be appropriate for research and development services, particularly with nonprofit educational institutions or other nonprofit organizations, and for facilities contracts.

Cost-Plus-Fixed-Fee

A cost-plus-fixed-fee contract is a cost-reimbursement contract that provides for payment to the supplier of a negotiated fee fixed at the inception of the contract. The fixed fee does not vary with actual cost, but may be adjusted as a result of the changes in the work to be performed under the contract. In order to permit such alterations the contract should contain a changes article or other mechanism specifically set forth in the contract for that purpose.

As a cost-reimbursement contract, cost-plus-fixed-fee provides for payment of allowable incurred costs to the extent prescribed in the contract. These contracts establish an estimate of total cost to obligate funds, determine the fixed fee, and establish a ceiling that the supplier may not exceed (except at its own risk) without a modification to the contract.

A cost-plus-fixed-fee contract may be useful in the following circumstances:

1. A contract for performing research or preliminary exploration or study when the level of effort to be required is unknown; or
2. A contract for development and testing when using a cost-plus-incentive-fee contract is not practical.

Cost-Plus-Incentive-Fee

A cost-plus-incentive-fee contract provides for a target cost, a target fee, a minimum and maximum fee, and a fee-adjustment formula. The buyer reimburses the supplier for all actual allowable costs and then applies the fee-adjustment formula. If the actual allowable costs exceed the target costs, applying the formula decreases the supplier's fee so that it is less than the target fee. If the actual allowable costs are less than the target costs, applying the formula increases the supplier's fee so that it is greater than the target fee. In other words, the lower the supplier's costs, the higher the supplier's fee and vice versa. The contract will not earn more than the maximum fee or less than the minimum fee regardless of costs incurred. Performance incentives may be applied to the contract arrangement to supplement the cost incentive, if appropriate.

The cost-plus-incentive-fee contract is suitable for use in development and test programs when cost (and performance) incentives are likely to motivate the supplier.

Cost-Plus-Award-Fee

The cost-plus-award-fee contract is a cost-reimbursement contract that provides for a fee consisting of a base amount fixed at inception of the contract plus an award that the supplier may earn in whole or in part during performance. The total earnable award should be large enough to motivate the supplier to excellence. The amount of the total earnable award actually paid is determined by the supplier's performance. Performance criteria are generally subjective measures of quality, timeliness, technical ingenuity, and cost-effective management, and are stated in the contract.

The cost-plus-award-fee contract is suitable for use when the following occurs:

1. Due to the nature of the contract work, it is neither feasible nor effective to devise predetermined objective incentive targets for cost, technical performance, or schedule.
2. The purchasing objective is more likely to be met using a contract with an incentive arrangement to motivate the supplier toward exceptional performance while providing the buyer with the flexibility to evaluate both actual performance and the conditions under which it was achieved.
3. Any additional administrative effort and cost required to monitor and evaluate performance are justified by the expected benefits.

"Hybrid" Contract Types

Time-and-Materials

Time-and-materials contracts are often used in service contracting. They have both fixed-price and cost-reimbursement characteristics. They provide for acquiring supplies or services on the basis of the following:

1. Direct labor hours at specified fixed hourly rates, which include wages, overhead, general and administrative expenses, and profit; **plus**
2. Materials at cost, including material handling costs only if appropriate.

A time-and-materials contract is not appropriate unless it is not possible at the time the contract is placed to estimate either the extent, duration or costs for performing the work with any reasonable degree of confidence.

A time-and-materials contract should be used when the following occurs:

1. No other contract type is suitable; and
2. The contract includes a separate ceiling for total labor costs beyond which the fixed hourly rates specified in the contract will be reduced. (Reducing the hourly labor rates is accomplished by deleting the profit included therein and is done to avoid a cost-plus-a-percentage-of-cost situation.)

Labor-Hour
Labor-hour contracts are a variation of the time-and-materials contract, differing only in that use of materials is not contemplated or is insignificant.

Combination Contracts
The buyer will be confronted with many situations that call for a flexible approach to structuring contracts. Many functions require considering combination or composite contracts. It is not uncommon to be confronted with a situation in which a combination firm-fixed-price/requirements/time-and-materials contract would be most effective. This is particularly true when a contract must incorporate both service and construction work. Many contracting situations call for work as needed, which essentially means the contract needs an indefinite-delivery type or time-and-materials/labor-hour type schedule of on-call requirements (often in conjunction with firm-fixed-price work).

Combining different types of contracts for associated services into a single contract document is practical. It reduces the number of formal solicitation packages that must be prepared, the solicitation effort, and the resulting contract documents.

Composite Contract Example: Building Maintenance
and Repair
Situation: The building maintenance service requirements are firm and definite. Substantial historical experience is available to establish the scope and level of maintenance required. The building repair service requirements are

sporadic and fluctuate to a large degree. Moreover, the repair services must be performed by construction tradesmen.

The buyer knows the following:

a. The nature of the work: the maintenance and repairs can be defined.
b. The amount of maintenance work based on historical data.
c. An estimate of the amount of repair work based on historical data.
d. Sound cost estimates for maintenance work and less-firm estimates for repair work can be established.

The buyer does not know the following:

a. When the repair work will be needed.
b. What specific types of repair will be ordered.
c. The exact number of buildings to be repaired.

Appropriate contract type: Combination of firm-fixed-price and time-and-materials
Why: The maintenance work to be performed can be defined and adequately described for a firm-fixed-price line item. The repair work, however, is not definite either in the quantity or frequency needed. It would not be reasonable to develop discrete, firm-fixed-price work unit line items for the repair work. The fact that the repair work must be done by construction tradesmen provides an added incentive to separate it from the maintenance work.

Agreements

Letter Contract
A letter contract is a preliminary written contractual instrument that authorizes the supplier to begin performing services immediately. Their use should be strictly discouraged.

Blanket Agreement
A blanket agreement is a written instrument of understanding that contains the elements shown in Table 4-6.

A blanket agreement is not a contract. Blanket agreements are used to avoid writing numerous purchase orders. They are appropriate, for example, if there is a wide variety of items in a broad class of services or goods that are generally purchased but the exact items, quantities, and delivery requirements are not known in advance and may vary considerably. A ceiling must be established for the total instrument as well as for each order (call).

TABLE 4-6   Elements of a blanket agreement.

Terms and conditions applying to future orders (calls) between the parties during its term.
A description, as specific as practicable, of deliverables to be provided.
Methods of pricing, issuing, and delivering future orders (calls) under the blanket order.

The automated contract preparation systems mentioned at the beginning of this chapter will help assure the buyer that the contract provisions have been tailored so that they are proper for the type of contract used and the category of services procured.

SUMMARY

The following elements are necessary to a good service contract.

1. A lucid description of work,
2. When and where the work will be performed,
3. Quantity ordered and price to be paid,
4. Payment terms and funding provisions,
5. Contract term (length),
6. Provisions for contract extensions and changes,
7. Quality control and inspection procedures,
8. Terms and conditions (provisions) that allocate risk,
9. Dispute resolution procedures,
10. Choice of law and legal forum for litigation, and
11. Termination procedures.

Creating different compensation arrangements to fit different situations has resulted in a variety of contract types. The benefits of using a more complex compensation arrangement must always be weighed against the cost of administering a more complex contract.

The following contract types are listed in order of preference.

Fixed-Price Family

Use when the work, the amount of work, and a base unit price can be predetermined precisely.

1. *Firm-fixed-price*: This is the contract of choice. Unit prices and total price are both immutable. Few circumstances make another contract type preferable.

2. *Fixed-price with economic price adjustment or escalation*: The fixed price will be adjusted if economic conditions alter supplier costs as measured or estimated in some predetermined fashion. It is often used when the supplier refuses to bear the risk of a firm-fixed-price contract in the face of expected fluctuations in economic conditions.

3. *Fixed-price incentive*: This is a fixed-price contract with incentive payments; the price is adjusted due to performance above or below set target(s). It is used when incentives are deemed necessary to gain the performance level desired for a reasonable total cost.

Indefinite-Delivery Type (IDT)

Use when unit prices can be predetermined but the timing and/or the amount of work cannot. There are two IDT contract types in general use for service contracting:

1. *Indefinite-quantity/indefinite-delivery (IQID)*: A minimum quantity is guaranteed; the supplier is not required to perform beyond a stated maximum quantity or dollar value. The supplier requires a guaranteed minimum to break even on high start-up costs.

2. *Requirements contracts*: A maximum quantity or dollar value and an estimated quantity are stated to help the supplier estimate unit costs preparatory to making an offer. No minimum quantity is guaranteed.

Cost-Reimbursement Family

Use when the work can be defined in rough terms but unit prices cannot. Usually economic or contract conditions contributing to supplier costs are so unstable that no reputable supplier will accept a fixed price. Supplier cost accounting systems must be able to deliver information adequate for reimbursement of costs.

1. *Cost no-fee/cost sharing*: No fee is paid. The supplier is generally a nonprofit organization.

2. *Cost-plus-fixed-fee*: The supplier's fee (profit) is fixed. Costs are extremely unstable and the supplier is generally a profit-making entity that does not need added incentives to preform adequately within a reasonable cost range.

3. *Cost-plus-incentive-fee*: Incentive payments are based on objective criteria. Use this type if the supplier needs such payments to perform adequately within a reasonable total cost range.

4. *Cost-plus-award-fee*: Incentive payments are based on subjective criteria.

The supplier needs such payments to perform adequately within a reasonable total cost range.

Hybrid Contract Types

1. *Time-and-materials*: The supplier is paid for direct labor at fixed hourly rates and materials at cost. Extent, duration and cost of the work cannot be predetermined. The contract should contain a ceiling price.
2. *Labor-hour*: The supplier is paid fixed hourly rates for direct labor. Material use is insignificant.
3. *Combination contracts*: Two or more of the above contract types operate together in one written instrument.

Agreements

1. *Letter contract*: This instrument authorizes the supplier to begin performing services before a final contract has been negotiated.
2. *Blanket agreement*: Using blanket agreements avoids the need for numerous purchase orders.

5

The Service Contract Solicitation

The solicitation is an offeror-oriented document. It is designed for two major purposes:

1. To guide and direct potential offerors in their preparation of priced proposals and offers.
2. To communicate those terms and conditions that will become part of the resulting contract.

There are many ways to satisfy these requirements, with each approach resulting in a different solicitation configuration. Regardless of the configuration, solicitations must include the elements listed in Table 5-1.

ELEMENTS OF THE SOLICITATION

The statement of work was covered thoroughly in chapter 3. A more complete description of the other elements of the solicitation follows.

TABLE 5-1   Elements of the service contract solicitation.

The statement of work.
A cover sheet.
A contract schedule of prices.
A specimen contract containing terms and conditions specific to service purchasing.
Pertinent specifications, drawings, and other appropriate technical data.
Instructions to offerors.

The Cover Sheet

The cover sheet should contain an explanation of the solicitation document structure. In some public-sector purchasing organizations the cover sheet serves multiple purposes: the top of the form is used by the buyer as a solicitation, the middle of the form is used by the service supplier to communicate the offer, the bottom of the form is used by the buyer to accept the offer.

A Contract Schedule of Prices

If the contract is a combination or composite type contract (often the case in service contracting), several types of schedules will be required.

Specimen Contract Terms and Conditions

Solicitation forms that fail to communicate the proposed contract format can complicate the process of arriving at mutually acceptable terms and conditions. Most organizations provide potential offerors with some type of specimen contract. A specimen contract contains a preoffer and prenegotiation version of what the buyer believes the final contract will be like, including the buying organization's desired terms and conditions.

In the federal sector, sections A through I of the "Uniform Contract Format" solicitation document constitute a specimen contract. The remainder of the solicitation (sections K, L, and M) is comprised of representations and certifications, instructions to offerors, and the evaluation criteria that will be used in selecting the successful service supplier. Many other organizations use standard solicitation forms that include instructions to offerors and other solicitation provisions. The statement of work, any necessary representations and certifications, standard terms and conditions for the type of contract being proposed, and the specimen contract are then attached to the solicitation form.

A sample specimen contract for a typical service purchase is attached as Appendix G.

Terms and conditions generally found in service contracts are often called "boilerplate." Because of their labor intensive nature, service terms and conditions are considerably different from those found in supply contracts. The following are examples.

Inspection of Services
This contract provision is absolutely essential. It spells out buyer obligations for receipt and inspection of contract deliverables. It should also spell out the

rights of the buyer whenever the service supplier fails to perform the required services or performs them in an unsatisfactory manner. Great specificity is required in describing actual or liquidated damages that might be levied against the nonconforming service supplier. Inspection provisions need to be tailored to the specific circumstances. A typical example follows.

(a) Definitions. "Services," as used in this clause, includes services performed, workmanship, and material furnished or utilized in the performance of services.

(b) The Supplier shall provide and maintain an inspection system acceptable to the Company covering the services under this Contract. Complete records of all inspection work performed by the Supplier shall be maintained and made available to the Company during contract performance and for as long afterwards as the contract requires.

(c) The Company has the right to inspect and test all services called for by the contract, to the extent practicable at all times and places during the term of the contract. The Company shall perform inspections and tests in a manner that will not unduly delay the work.

(d) If any of the services do not conform with contract requirements, the Company may require the Supplier to perform the services again in conformity with contract requirements, at no increase in contract amount. When the defects in services cannot be corrected by reperformance, the Company may:

　(1) require the Supplier to take necessary action to ensure that future performance conforms to contract requirements, and

　(2) reduce the contract price to reflect the reduced value of the services performed.

(e) If the Supplier fails to promptly perform the services again or to take the necessary action to ensure future performance in conformity with contract requirements, the Company may:

　(1) by contract or otherwise, perform the services and charge to the Supplier any cost incurred by the Company that is directly related to the performance of such service, or

　(2) terminate the contract for default.

Key Personnel

This contract provision clearly states that the individuals whose names and titles are listed are considered critical to the success of the contract. Their reassignment or removal from the project will be subject to buyer approval. The following is typical of a key personnel provision.

The personnel specified in an attachment to this Contract are considered to be essential to the work being performed hereunder. Prior to diverting any of the specified individuals to other programs, the Supplier shall notify the Buyer reasonably in advance and shall submit justification (including proposed substitutions) in sufficient detail to permit evaluation of the impact on the program. No diversion shall be made by the Buyer:

Provided, that the Buyer may ratify in writing such diversion and such ratification shall constitute the consent of the Buyer required by this clause. The attachment to this Contract may be amended from time to time during the course of the contract to either add or delete personnel, as appropriate.

Continuity of Services

This contract provision requires the incumbent service supplier to furnish phase-in training to its successor for a stated number of days after contract termination, and to exercise best efforts to cooperate in an orderly and efficient transition. Contracts generally use a separate line item for this provision. The following provision is typical.

(a) The Supplier recognizes that the services under this Contract are vital to the Company and must be continued without interruption and that upon contract expiration, a successor, either the Company or another supplier, may continue them. The Supplier agrees to:
  (1) furnish phase-in training, and
  (2) exercise its best efforts and cooperation to effect an orderly and efficient transition to a successor.

(b) The Supplier shall, upon the Buyer's written notice,
  (1) furnish phase-in, phase-out services for up to 60 days after this Contract expires, and
  (2) negotiate in good faith a plan with a successor to determine the nature and extent of phase-in, phase-out services required. The plan shall specify a training program and a date for transferring responsibilities for each division of work described in the plan, and shall be subject to the Buyer's approval. The Supplier shall provide sufficient experienced personnel during the phase-in, phase-out period to ensure that the services called for by this Contract are maintained at the required level of proficiency.

(c) The Supplier shall allow as many personnel as practicable to remain on the job to help the successor maintain the continuity and consistency of the services required by this Contract. The Supplier also shall disclose necessary personnel records and allow the successor to conduct on-site interviews with these employees. If selected employees are agreeable to the change, the Supplier shall release them at a mutually agreeable date and negotiate transfer of their earned fringe benefits to the successor.

(d) The Supplier shall be reimbursed for all reasonable phase-in, phase-out costs (that is, costs incurred within the agreed period after contract expiration that result from phase-in, phase-out operations) and a fee (profit) not to exceed a pro rata portion of the fee (profit) under this Contract.

Ordering

This contract provision, generally required for non–firm-fixed-price contracts, provides a mechanism for ordering services throughout the term of the contract. A typical example follows.

(a) Any supplies and services to be furnished under this contract shall be ordered by issuance of delivery orders by the individuals or activities designated in the Schedule. Such orders may be issued from _____ through _____.

(b) All delivery orders are subject to the terms and conditions of this Contract. In the event of conflict between a delivery order and this contract, the contract shall control.

(c) If mailed, a delivery order is considered "issued" when the Company deposits the order in the mail. Orders may be issued orally or by written telecommunications only if authorized in the Schedule.

Order Limitations

An "order limitations" provision should be included whenever an ordering provision is included in a contract. It spells out the minimum and maximum order quantities to which the supplier will be contractually required to respond. The following is a typical example.

(a) Minimum order. When the Company requires supplies or services covered by this Contract in an amount of less than _____, the Company is not obligated to purchase, nor is the Supplier obligated to furnish, those supplies or services under the contract.

(b) Maximum order. The Supplier is not obligated to honor:
  (1) Any order for a single item in excess of _____;
  (2) Any order for a combination of items in excess of _____; or
  (3) A series of orders from the same ordering office within _____ days that together call for quantities exceeding the limitations in subparagraph (1) or (2) above.

(c) If this is a requirements contract (that is, includes the Requirements clause), the Company is not required to order a part of any one requirement from the Supplier if that requirement exceeds the maximum-order limitations in paragraph (b) above.

(d) Notwithstanding paragraphs (b) and (c) above, the Supplier shall honor any order exceeding the maximum order limitations in paragraph (b), unless that order (or orders) is returned to the ordering office within _____ days after issuance, with written notice stating the Supplier's intent not to supply the service (or services) called for and the reasons. Upon receiving this notice, the Company may acquire the supplies or services from another source.

Requirements

A "requirements" provision is used in requirements contracts to explain how the contract operates. It should state clearly that the quantities in the schedule are merely estimates, that buyer requirements will be ordered as they become evident under the ordering provision and the order limitation provision. A ceiling amount should also be included, either in the requirements provision or an accompanying revision. The following is a typical example:

(a) This is a requirements contract for the supplies or services specified, and effective for the period stated in the Schedule. The quantities of supplies or services specified in the Schedule are estimates only and are not purchased by this Contract. Except as this Contract may otherwise provide, if the Company's requirements do not result in orders in the quantities described as "estimated" or "maximum" in the Schedule, that fact shall not constitute the basis for an equitable price adjustment.

(b) Delivery or performance shall be made only as authorized by orders issued in accordance with the Ordering clause. Subject to any limitations in the Delivery-Order Limitations clause or elsewhere in this contract, the Supplier shall furnish to the Company all supplies or services specified in the Schedule and called for by orders issued in accordance with the Ordering clause. The Company may issue orders requiring delivery to multiple destinations or performance at multiple locations.

(c) Except as this Contract otherwise provides, the Company shall order from the Supplier all the supplies or services specified in the Schedule that are required to be purchased by the Company activity or activities specified in the Schedule.

(d) The Company is not required to purchase from the Supplier requirements in excess of any limit on total orders under this Contract.

(e) If the Company urgently requires delivery of any quantity of an item before the earliest date that delivery may be specified under this Contract, and if the Supplier will not accept an order providing for the accelerated delivery, the Company may acquire the urgently required goods or services from another source.

(f) Any order issued during the effective period of this contract and not completed within that period shall be completed by the Supplier within the time specified in the order. The contract shall govern the Supplier's and Company's rights and obligations with respect to that order to the same extent as if the order were completed during the contract's effective period; provided, that the Supplier shall not be required to make any deliveries under this Contract after _____.

Indefinite-Quantity

An "indefinite-quantity" provision is used in IQID contracts to explain how the contract operates. They are similar to the requirements provisions in many respects. They should state clearly that the quantities in the schedule are estimates only and that they are not actually being purchased by the contract. They should spell out that buyer requirements, as they become evident, will be ordered under the ordering provision and the order limitation provision. A ceiling amount should be included in the indefinite quantity provision or in a companion provision. Unlike requirements provisions, indefinite-quantity provisions should clarify the fact that the minimum quantity/value specified in the schedule will be guaranteed. Many organizations have a policy, stated in either this provision or an accompanying one, that the minimum quantity or value will be ordered during the current fiscal year.

(a) This is an indefinite-quantity contract for the supplies or services specified, and effective for the period stated, in the Schedule. The quantities of supplies and services specified in the Schedule are estimates only and are not purchased by this Contract.

(b) Delivery or performance shall be made only as authorized by orders issued in accordance with the Ordering clause. The Supplier shall furnish to the Company, when and if ordered, the supplies or services specified in the Schedule up to and including the quantity designated in the Schedule as the "maximum." The Company shall order at least the quantity of supplies or services designated in the Schedule as the "minimum."

(c) Except for any limitations on quantities in the Delivery-Order Limitations clause or in the Schedule, there is no limit on the number of orders that may be issued. The Company may issue orders requiring delivery to multiple destinations or performance at multiple locations.

(d) Any order issued during the effective period of this Contract and not completed within that period shall be completed by the Supplier within the time specified in the order. The contract shall govern the Supplier's and Company's rights and obligations with respect to that order to the same extent as if the order were completed during the contract's effective period; provided, that the Supplier shall not be required to make any deliveries under this Contract after _____.

Option to Extend the Term of the Contract

Service contracts are generally written in a multiple-year format. This is usually achieved by specifying a base period (generally twelve months) and a number of option periods. This contract provision should state the length of the base period, the length of the option periods, and the number of option periods that may be added to the contract term solely at the option of the buyer. Three to five years is an average contract term: one base year with two to four one-year option periods. A typical extension option follows.

(a) The Company may extend the term of this Contract by written notice to the Supplier within _____; provided, that the Company shall give the

Supplier a preliminary written notice of its intent to extend at least 60 days before the contract expires. The preliminary notice does not commit the Company to an extension.
(b) If the Company exercises this option, the extended contract shall be considered to include this option provision.
(c) The total duration of this Contract, including the exercise of any options under this clause, shall not exceed _____.

Suspension of Work, Delay of Work, and Stop-Work Order

Provisions of this nature are required to suspend, delay, or stop work. They should make clear the respective rights and responsibilities of the buyer and service supplier, particularly with respect to the cost and schedule impact of these actions. Typical examples follow.

Suspension of Work

(a) The Buyer may order the Supplier, in writing, to suspend, delay, or interrupt all or any part of the work of this Contract for the period of time that the Buyer determines appropriate for the convenience of the Company.
(b) If the performance of all or any part of the work is, for an unreasonable period of time, suspended, delayed, or interrupted
   (1) by an act of the Buyer in the administration of this Contract, or
   (2) by the Buyer's failure to act within the time specified in this Contract (or within a reasonable time if not specified), an adjustment shall be made for any increase in the cost of performance of this contract (excluding profit) necessarily caused by the unreasonable suspension, delay, or interruption, and the contract modified in writing accordingly. However, no adjustment shall be made under this clause for any suspension, delay, or interruption to the extent that performance would have been so suspended, delayed, or interrupted by any other cause, including the fault or negligence of the Supplier, or for which an equitable adjustment is provided for or excluded under any other term or condition of this Contract.
(c) A claim under this clause shall not be allowed
   (1) for any costs incurred more than 20 days before the Supplier shall have notified the Buyer in writing of the act or failure to act involved (but this requirement shall not apply as to a claim resulting from a suspension order), and
   (2) unless the claim, in an amount stated, is asserted in writing as soon as practicable after the termination of the suspension, delay, or interruption, but not later than the date of final payment under the contract.

Delay of Work

(a) If the performance of all or any part of the work of this Contract is delayed or interrupted

    (1) by an act of the Buyer in the administration of this Contract that is not expressly or implicitly authorized by this Contract, or

    (2) by a failure of the Buyer to act within the time specified in this Contract, or within a reasonable time if not specified, an adjustment (excluding profit) shall be made for any increase in the cost of performance of this Contract caused by the delay or interruption and the contract shall be modified in writing accordingly. Adjustment shall also be made in the delivery or performance dates and any other contractual term or condition affected by the delay or interruption. However, no adjustment shall be made under this clause for any delay or interruption to the extent that performance would have been delayed or interrupted by any other cause, including the fault or negligence of the Supplier, or for which an adjustment is provided or excluded under any other term or condition of this Contract.

(b) A claim under this clause shall not be allowed

    (1) for any costs incurred more than 20 days before the Supplier shall have notified the Buyer in writing of the act or failure to act involved, and

    (2) unless the claim, in an amount stated, is asserted in writing as soon as practicable after the termination of the delay or interruption, but not later than the day of final payment under the contract.

Stop-Work Order

(a) The Buyer may, at any time, by written order to the Supplier, require the Supplier to stop all, or any part, of the work called for by this Contract for a period of 90 days after the order is delivered to the Supplier, and for any further period to which the parties may agree. The order shall be specifically identified as a stop-work order issued under this clause. Upon receipt of the order, the Supplier shall immediately comply with its terms and take all reasonable steps to minimize the incurrence of costs allocable to the work covered by the order during the period of work stoppage. Within a period of 90 days after a stop-work is delivered to the Supplier, or within any extension of that period to which the parties shall have agreed, the Buyer shall either—

    (1) Cancel the stop-work order; or

    (2) Terminate the work covered by the order as provided in the Default, or the Termination for Convenience of the Company, clause of this Contract.

(b) If a stop-work order issued under this clause is canceled or the period of the order or any extension thereof expires, the Supplier shall resume work. The Buyer shall make an equitable adjustment in the delivery schedule or contract price, or both, and the contract shall be modified, in writing, accordingly, if—

   (1) The stop-work order results in an increase in the time required for, or in the Supplier's cost properly allocable to, the performance of any part of this Contract; and

   (2) The Supplier asserts its right to the adjustment within 30 days after the end of the period of work stoppage; provided, that, if the Buyer decides the facts justify the action, the Buyer may receive and act upon the claim submitted at any time before final payment under this contract.

  (c) If a stop-work order is not canceled and the work covered by the order is terminated for the convenience of the Company, the Buyer shall allow reasonable costs resulting from the stop-work order in arriving at the termination settlement.

  (d) If a stop-work order is not canceled and the work covered by the order is terminated for default, the Buyer shall allow, by equitable adjustment or otherwise, reasonable costs resulting from the stop-work order.

Warranty of Services

A warranty provision is often a necessary supplement to an "inspection of services" provision. Although warranty periods for services should logically be shorter than those for supplies, the buyer usually has a right to require the service supplier to stand behind his or her work for an agreed-upon period of time. Quite obviously, this period should vary with the type and nature of the services. Consultants, for example, will generally not accept any period of warranty unless they are supplying design services. The buyer should always be aware that warranties are not free. The longer the warranty period required, the more the buyer must pay. A typical provision follows:

  (a) Definitions. "Acceptance," as used in this clause, means the act of an authorized representative of the Company by which the Company assumes for itself, or as an agent of another, ownership of existing and identified supplies, or approves specific services, as partial or complete performance of the contract. "Correction," as used in this clause, means the elimination of a defect.

  (b) Notwithstanding inspection and acceptance by the Company or any provision concerning the conclusiveness thereof, the Supplier warrants that all services performed under this Contract will, at the time of acceptance, be free from defects in workmanship and conform to the requirements of this Contract. The Buyer shall give written notice of any defect or non-conformance to the Supplier. This notice shall state either:

   (1) that the Supplier shall correct or reperform any defective or nonconforming services, or

   (2) that the Company does not require correction or reperformance.

  (c) If the Supplier is required to correct or reperform, it shall be at no cost to the Company, and any services corrected or reperformed by the Supplier shall be subject to this clause to the same extent as work initially performed. If the Supplier fails or refuses to correct or reperform, the Buyer may, by contract or otherwise, correct or replace with similar services and charge to the Supplier the cost occasioned to the Company thereby, or make an equitable adjustment in the contract price.

(d) If the Company does not require correction or reperformance, the Buyer shall make an equitable adjustment in the contract price.

Terms and Conditions Not Included in the Boilerplate

It is almost a maxim that service contracts must be tailored to the circumstances. The vast majority of service contracts must supplement and modify the standard terms and conditions. Situations requiring special terms are many and varied. If buyer property will be provided (not typical in service contracts), or if the contract will be set aside for specific socioeconomic groups, supplemental provisions will be necessary.

Specifications, Drawings, and Other Appropriate Technical Data

Although it is advisable to avoid the use of separate specifications and drawings in service contracts, contracts dealing with construction or facility maintenance and repair almost always require such documents.

Instructions to Offerors

A section containing specific instructions and guidance to potential offerors is generally advisable. It should specify the criteria that the buyer will use in arriving at an award decision; the requirements for preparing and submitting management, technical, and cost/business proposals; representations and certifications; and any small-disadvantaged business plan requirements as well as other pertinent guidance the potential offerors will need to be responsive to the solicitation.

A sample solicitation for a typical service procurement is attached as Appendix F.

SUMMARY

The solicitation has two major purposes:

1. To direct potential offerors as they prepare their offers.
2. To communicate the terms and conditions that will become part of the final contract.

Solicitations must include the following:

1. The statement of work;
2. A cover sheet;
3. A contract schedule of prices;
4. Terms and conditions specific to service purchasing;
5. Pertinent specifications, drawings, and other appropriate technical data;
6. Instructions to offerors.

6

The Service Contract Evaluation and Selection Process

In public-sector contracting, service suppliers are generally selected on a sealed bid (formal advertising) basis. In the private sector, competitive bidding, generally without a public opening of bids, is the preferred procurement method. Firm-fixed-price contracting with the lowest responsive and responsible bidder is attempted and often achieved in both public and private sectors. Some industries and firms in the public arena know no other way. This is particularly true of the construction business.

Price/cost should always be a factor in selecting service suppliers, but it may not be the most important factor. Service purchases often provide more opportunity and present more challenges than supply purchases, making it appropriate and/or necessary to deviate from the strict firm-fixed-price after advertising mode of selection. For example, the organization may want to award a contract to the service supplier with the highest affordable technical quality, but may not be able to define that level of quality with sufficient specificity for the statement of work. In such cases a "best-value" evaluation approach permits the organization to request technical (and other) proposals, from which the level of quality can be inferred. Other textbooks on purchasing deal extensively with the process of competitive bidding. Although this book recognizes the importance of competitive bidding, even in service purchasing, it will concentrate on an explanation of a process recommended for use in accommodating selection factors in addition to price.

In many service procurements, it is highly appropriate to use a logical mix of technical/management and price/cost/business evaluation criteria in selecting a firm. Typically, the more technical the work, the more weight the technical criteria are given. Treatment of price/cost in evaluating architect–engineering or research and development proposals serves as an example of the highly technical end of the service spectrum. Although some firms have recently begun considering price and technical factors simultaneously, it is still industrywide practice to consider price/cost in procuring architect/engineering (design) services only after an initial selection based on technical qualifications. Purchasing research and development services often warrants consideration of price/cost only if offerors are otherwise equally technically qualified. Consultants are almost always selected on technical qualifications, as long as the rate of compensation doesn't exceed preestablished policy parameters.

Price analysis must be used at some point in every procurement, regardless of the procurement method, to determine if the price is reasonable. Generally the buyer conducts the price analysis without outside assistance. When price analysis alone cannot assure a fair and reasonable price, the buyer should anticipate the need for cost data and request such data in the solicitation. When cost data is required, the buyer must coordinate the analysis of the cost proposal or cost data submitted by the service supplier. The results of the price and/or cost analysis are necessary in price negotiations with the supplier.

PRICE ANALYSIS

Price analysis is the process of examining and evaluating a proposed price without evaluating either the separate cost elements or the level of profit which combine to yield the price. It may be accomplished by the following comparisons, which are listed in Table 6-1, in order of their ease of use. The buyer should choose the method or methods that will yield acceptable results.

TABLE 6-1   Price analysis methodologies.

Comparison with other prices and quotations submitted.

Comparison with published catalog or market prices of commercial items sold in substantial quantities to the general public.

Comparison with prices set by law or regulation (for regulated industries).

Comparison with prices for the same or similar items.

Comparison with prior quotations for the same or similar items.

Comparison with market data (indexes).

Application of rough yardsticks (such as dollars per pound or per horsepower or other units) to highlight significant inconsistencies that warrant additional pricing inquiry.

Comparison with independent estimates of cost developed by knowledgeable personnel within the buyer organization.

Use of value analysis.

Use of visual analysis.

COST ANALYSIS

Cost analysis is the review and evaluation of (a) the separate cost elements and proposed profit/fee of an offeror's cost or pricing data, and (b) the judgmental factors the offeror applied in projecting from that data to the estimated costs for supplying the service. The purpose of cost analysis is to form an opinion on the degree of validity to assign to the offeror's cost estimates, assuming reasonable economy and efficiency. Verifying cost data and evaluating cost elements should include the following:

1. Evaluation of the necessity for and reasonableness of proposed costs.
2. Projection of the offeror's cost trends on the basis of current and historical cost data (that is, estimates of inflation or deflation and learning curve effects).
3. A technical appraisal of the offeror's estimates of labor, material, tooling and facilities requirements and of the reasonableness of scrap and spoilage factors.
4. Evaluation of the application of audited or negotiated indirect cost rates, labor rates, or other factors.

Where the necessary data are available, the offeror's current estimated costs should be compared with the items in Table 6-2.

Cost analysis should not be employed when reasonableness of price can be established by the following:

1. Established catalog or market prices of commercial items sold to the general public in substantial quantities,
2. Prices set by law or regulation, or
3. The presence of adequate price competition.

Definitions
   Adequate Price Competition   Adequate price competition exists if offers are solicited with the following results:

TABLE 6-2   Items to compare against offeror's estimated costs.

Actual costs previously incurred by the same supplier or offeror.
Previous cost estimates from the offeror or from other offerors for the same or similar items.
Other cost estimates received in response to the solicitation.
Independent cost estimates by technical personnel.
Forecasts of planned expenditures.

1. Two or more responsible offerors who are able to satisfy the solicitation requirements respond to the solicitation's expressed requirements.
2. These offerors compete independently for a contract to be awarded to the responsible offeror submitting the lowest evaluated price.

Price must be a substantial factor in the evaluation and the award must be based on price analysis alone. A price may be justified on the basis of adequate price competition if the following applies:

1. It results directly from price competition; or
2. Price analysis alone clearly demonstrates that the proposed price is reasonable compared with current or recent prices for the same or substantially the same items purchased in comparable quantities, with comparable terms and conditions, under contracts that resulted from adequate price competition.

Established Catalog Prices   Established catalog prices are those prices included in a catalog, price list, schedule, or other form the supplier regularly publishes or otherwise maintains for customer inspection, and which states prices at which sales are currently being made to a significant number of buyers constituting the general public. The item must be a commercial item sold in substantial quantities to the general public in the course of conducting normal business operations. This method may also be used for items sufficiently similar to such commercial items to permit the differences in prices to be identified and justified without resort to cost analysis.

Established Market Prices   Established market prices are current prices established in the course of ordinary and usual trade between buyers and sellers free to bargain and that can be substantiated without recourse to data supplied by the offeror.

NONPRICE SELECTION CRITERIA (BEST-VALUE SOURCE SELECTION)

When factors other than price/cost are included in the evaluation criteria and those criteria can be defined adequately, the organization often follows a process like that in Table 6-3.

An explanation of the various aspects of Best-Value source selection follows.

TABLE 6-3   The process for source selection using nonprice criteria.

An advance purchasing plan is developed.
A source-selection plan is developed.
Offers are solicited using a written solicitation.
Technical/management and price/cost/business proposals are submitted.
Proposals are evaluated and scored.
A competitive range for negotiation is determined. If two or more proposals are fully acceptable and price competition is present, award is made. If negotiations are required for technical and/or cost reasons, the process continues.
If discussions are to be held, all offerors are notified of their status either inside or outside the competitive range.
Offerors within the competitive range are invited to discussions and advised of their deficiencies.
Offerors remaining within the competitive range are invited to submit best and final offers (BAFOs).
A final evaluation is made and final scores determined.
Final evaluation results are presented to the source-selection official (usually the buyer).
The source-selection official makes an award decision.
The buyer awards a contract and notifies unsuccessful offerors.
Unsuccessful offerors are briefed upon request.

The Best-Value Advance Purchasing Plan

See chapter 2 for directions on developing an Advance Purchasing Plan.

The Best-Value Source Selection Plan

A best-value source-selection plan should be developed on a team basis and should contain the information in Table 6-4.

Soliciting Offerors Using Best-Value Source Selection

The buyer team should assure that the solicitation language clearly states the award evaluation factors and proposal-submittal requirements as spelled out in the source-selection plan. In accomplishing this, the team should assure the following:

1. The solicitation sections devoted to award evaluation criteria and proposal-submittal requirements, though kept separate, are highly correlated and not inconsistent with each other. (Each criterion must have a corresponding proposal submittal requirement.)

TABLE 6-4   Contents of a best-value source-selection plan.

The technical/management criteria/evaluation factors for award in their relative order of importance. (Include only factors that are important to the current source-selection decision.)
Proposal submittal requirements to which offerors may respond.
Procedures for selecting a technical/management review team.
Proposal evaluation procedures for use by the technical/management proposal review team.
Price/cost/business proposal evaluation procedures for use by the buyer.
Plans for contract negotiation, if appropriate.
Designation of the source-selection official (if other than the buyer).

2. The evaluation criteria are either listed in descending order of importance, or are weighted with the total adding up to 100 percent.
3. The proposal-submittal instructions contain a limit on the number of pages a proposal may have.
4. The proposal-submittal instructions clearly specify the number of proposal copies to be submitted.
5. The proposal-submittal instructions clearly specify that price/cost/business proposal level of detail should be limited to the highest practicable level of the work breakdown structure.
6. The proposal-submittal instructions require the technical/management and price/cost/business proposal volumes to be separate, distinct documents.

Evaluating Proposals in Best-Value Source Selection

If all potential service suppliers respond timely and in conformance with the terms of the solicitation, the next step in best-value source selection may begin. In this step the buying team must begin the evaluation process. Rating systems commonly used are listed in Table 6-5.

The evaluation works best when predetermined forms and procedures govern the process. These predetermined procedures generally call for the buyer to log in all proposals and then distribute the various sections to the evaluation team. Normally the buyer retains all copies of price/cost/business

TABLE 6-5   Common rating schemes for evaluating best value proposals.

Points are applied to supplier responses to evaluation factors.
Color coding is used to reflect categorization of quality of each supplier's response to specific evaluation criteria, with blue = exceptional, green = acceptable, yellow = marginal, and red = unacceptable.
Adjectival ratings structured around a three-, four-, six-, or ten-descriptor scoring system.

proposals plus one master copy of all other proposal volumes and releases the remaining copies of the technical and management proposals to the head of the technical/management evaluation team. After the head of this team distributes the technical and management proposals to team members, they conduct their evaluation. Normally the team uses the following procedures:

1. All members of the team review all proposals.
2. Members of the team use preprepared evaluation forms to rate the proposals.
   A workable ten-descriptor scoring system is presented below:

Adjectival Rating	Score	Adjectival Rating	Score
Outstanding	10	Weak	4
Superior	9	Poor	3
Excellent	8	Very poor	2
Very good	7	Inadequate	1
Good	6	Nonresponsive	0
Adequate	5		

Defining the Competitive Range for Best-Value Source Selection

After aggregating individual team member scores or ratings, the technical/management evaluation team chief must identify each proposal as being within one of the categories listed in Table 6-6.

Documenting Evaluation of Technical/Management Proposals

The technical/management team chief must document the team's findings in a memorandum to the buyer. Negotiations with the offerors cannot commence until the buyer receives this report. The report should sort each proposal into one of the three categories listed in Table 6-6 and state

TABLE 6-6   Categories of proposals in best-value source selection.

Proposal is acceptable as received.

Proposal might be brought to an acceptable status with a reasonable effort on the part of the buying organization and the service supplier.

Proposal is not acceptable—no further consideration warranted. Proposals in this category are so technically inadequate as to remove them from further consideration. Examples of such deficiencies are offering an approach previously found unworkable or offering an effort inconsistent with the stated objectives of the solicitation.

the results of the point evaluation, if conducted. In addition, the technical/management team chief should include a narrative evaluation specifying the strengths and weaknesses of each proposal and any reservations or qualifications that might bear on the selection of potential service suppliers for inclusion within the competitive range. Specific technical reasons supporting a determination that any proposal is unacceptable should also be included.

Cost Analysis in Best-Value Source Selection

The person responsible for evaluating and scoring price/cost/business proposals (if scoring is required by the evaluation plan in the source-selection plan) is always the buyer. Ordinarily only price analysis is involved since price competition will be present in most service procurements.

The buyer who has requested and received detailed cost proposals in the course of a best-value source selection will have some additional effort on his or her hands. In such cases the buyer will generally find it necessary to obtain technical evaluation input concerning the cost proposals. The technical/management review team can assist in determining whether the cost proposals reflect an adequate understanding of the work. Evaluating the direct cost elements can reveal whether the proposer has adequately provided for the required services, materials, equipment, travel, and other expenses. Another way of explaining this is that the cost proposal must provide a "mirror image" of the technical approach included in the technical proposal. Failure of the offeror to address areas of work in the cost proposal should cause the buyer to question whether the offeror really understands the work. This evaluation should address the following:

1. *The completeness of the supplier's proposed costs.* This assumes the supplier presented a work plan in its technical proposal. The degree to which the supplier correlates and allocates the labor, material, and other resources required in the cost proposal to the work plan in the technical proposal will directly influence the efficiency, productivity, and schedule compliance.
2. *Relationship of the proposed costs to the required work.* In this assessment, the technical/management team will determine whether all costs proposed are necessary for satisfactorily complete the work. Proposed costs for work determined to be unnecessary should be excluded.
3. *The degree to which proposed work elements are duplicated.* A given cost proposal may contain costs that have been listed elsewhere in the same proposal or in prior proposals for work that was completed prior to the current contract. Such duplications should be excluded from current costs.

4. *Validity of estimating techniques used in the proposal.* If historical data is used in projecting future cost, the team should determine if the current contract schedule, work load, and other conditions have been adequately considered as a basis for projecting historical costs into the future.
5. *The impact of schedule and work load.* This evaluation looks at the time period within which the contract work should be completed, and attempts to determine whether the total quantity of effort proposed is correct. The team will review the cost proposal to assure that there is a proper balance of manpower working on a task for the time span over which the task is to be performed.

If the cost/price analysis indicates the need for cost and price negotiations (as opposed to technical negotiations), the buyer will need the technical/management review team to provide a quantitative analysis of the offeror's quantities of labor, materials, and equipment. Buyer (or auditor)-developed unit cost rates can then be applied to the quantities of resources required in deriving a total cost position for negotiation. The quantitative analysis of the service supplier's cost proposal should determine the following:

1. *The appropriateness of the proposed skill level and mix.* This analysis is important because labor is generally the largest element of cost in service contracts. Part of understanding and evaluating estimated labor is to recognize the patterns in the incidence of different types of labor. Each phase of a work effort will have its own unique combination of required labor types. The skill, grade, and salary levels proposed must make sense when the phases are compared not only with the job as a whole, but with each other.
2. *The reasonableness of proposed direct labor hours.* This analysis attempts to determine whether the supplier has projected the proposed number of direct labor hours based on a sound plan that makes proper use of labor to achieve reasonable economy and efficiency of operation. The tests for labor-hour reasonableness will include consideration of the following:
   - the necessity of the proposed effort,
   - the adequacy of the work plan,
   - whether any work has been duplicated,
   - the applicability of historical data,
   - the conditions under which the work will be performed,
   - the estimating methods employed, and
   - the supplier's knowledge of the task. If the service supplier has performed similar services in the past, the supplier's personnel may manifest a classical learning curve. If so their productivity will be greater

than average on the instant contract because they learned how to do the job on earlier contracts. Learning is a universal phenomenon that applies to service contracts as well as supply contracts.

3. *Reasonableness of proposed material types and quantities.* Although not generally a major cost element in service contracts, material can be quite significant, particularly in construction and other facilities-related service contracts. Ideally, the supplier will have developed consolidated lists or bills of materials based in some way on existing plans and drawings. In that eventuality, the technical team can readily compare the quantity of proposed material with the quantity of material estimated on the detailed in-house estimate. In the absence of such plans, the supplier may have to rely solely on historical experience. Analysis of the supplier's estimate of material quantities should include a projection of a reasonable learning curve in materials usage. The learning curve phenomenon applies to use of materials as well as to labor.

4. *Reasonableness of other direct costs (quantities) proposed.* Other direct costs are those costs specifically identified with a project but that do not fall within the classification of either direct labor or direct material. Examples include equipment, subcontracts, travel, automatic data processing, consultants, and meetings and conferences. These direct costs are reviewed to determine whether the costs are properly classified in accordance with the supplier's accounting system, and whether the backup data in support of the costs are valid, current, and applicable to the work required.

5. *Reasonableness of the proposed profit or fee.* Although the technical team should not be asked to develop a recommended profit or fee, it can render an opinion on the inherent technical, management, and cost risk they perceive in the work as well as an opinion on the degree to which the supplier is willing to assume that risk. Generally, higher cost estimates (padding of cost, either in quantity or rates) evidence an unwillingness by the supplier to assume risk.

As indicated earlier, the buyer will need to develop unit cost rates (labor, material, equipment, overhead, G & A, and profit) that can be applied against the quantitative estimates of the technical/management evaluation team in order to derive a total cost position for negotiation. This analysis of the service supplier's cost proposal should include reasonableness of proposed labor rates, material costs, and other direct costs. A detailed explanation of these analyses follows.

The Reasonableness of Proposed Labor Rates

When analyzing cost proposals of incumbent firms, it is fairly simple to review historical payrolls and track specific employees to the proposal. Historical rates will, of course, be extrapolated to reflect salary increases in effect during the performance period. These increases must be reviewed in the light of past history and economic reasonableness before they are accepted. On service contracts that require the service supplier to acquire new employees, the offer letters may be reviewed to determine rates. Lacking this evidence, wage and salary survey information available from the American Management Association, the U.S. Department of Labor, and other sources can be consulted for reasonable, market-based rates in the area of contract performance. Labor rate analysis should generally include the following elements:

1. Determination of the adequacy of supplier-provided information.
2. Review of position descriptions and pay scales for currency.
3. Verification that salary rates are based on individual employee regular compensation.
4. Determination of the basis used to estimate salaries and evaluation of the salaries to determine reasonableness.
5. Determination that a weighted averaging process was used to determine proposed salaries (in the absence of specific identification of personnel).
6. Determination of the reasonableness of proposed salary escalation or inflation factors.
7. Review of labor included in both direct and indirect cost pools to assure there has been no double dipping by the supplier. (Vacation, holiday, and leave should be particularly scrutinized for potential double dipping.)
8. Review of labor classification systems to assure consistency in classification as direct or indirect.
9. Review of consultant and subcontractor labor costs to assure they have not been included in supplier direct labor categories.
10. Review of the supplier's cost-accounting system (particularly for other than firm-fixed-price contracts) to assure the system can properly allocate costs to jobs.

The Reasonableness of Proposed Material Prices

When analyzing incumbent firms' cost proposals, it is fairly simple to review books and records to track historical prices paid for proposed materials. If used as the basis for future cost estimates, these historical prices must be extrapolated to the period of contract performance using an appropriate price index. On service contracts with no previous incumbent experience, proposed material prices should be pegged to whatever published, catalog, or market prices are available in the literature. In conducting the material price analysis, the buyer (or auditor acting for the buyer) must assure that costs are consistently treated in accordance with the normal cost-keeping system of the supplier; that costs are traceable to and can be supported by such documentation as bills of materials, vendors' quotes, and subcontracts; and that costs are reasonable in view of actual prices, with appropriate adjustment for trade discounts, refunds, rebates, allowances, prompt payment, and so forth. Material price/rate analysis should generally include the following elements:

1. A review of a detailed, itemized, consolidated bill of materials submitted by the supplier. The supplier should be required to attach to this bill of materials documentation, including vendor quotations, purchase orders, or catalog extracts for high-dollar value items included on the bill.
2. Verification that material prices include all appropriate discounts, rebates, and allowances.
3. Determination of the reasonableness of scrap, spoilage, and return rates.
4. Verification that buyer-provided material is not included in the supplier cost proposal.
5. Assessment of the degree to which the supplier and subcontractors have used price competition in material purchases.
6. Review of material included in both direct and indirect cost pools to assure there has been no double dipping by the supplier.
7. Review of the supplier's cost-accounting system and proposal-preparation system to assure they are consistent.
8. Verification of the adequacy of the supplier's inventory management system and/or materials management system (MMS).

The Reasonableness of Proposed Other Direct Cost Prices/Rates

Other direct costs generally include a combination of different types of costs that include specialized labor, equipment, and support costs. The rates for these types of costs should be analyzed by pegging them wherever possible to the market and to past history and experience on the part of the service supplier and the buyer's organization. Analysis of other direct costs should generally include the following:

1. Verification that the service supplier's equipment notes are consistent with the supplier's property records and depreciation schedules.
2. Verification that the service supplier's leased equipment rates are consistent with established rates from Dataquest, the Association of General Contractors, and the U.S. Army Corps of Engineers.
3. Determination of whether subcontract costs are fair and reasonable. The supplier should be required to submit detailed subcontractor cost proposals for significantly sized subcontracts.

4. Verification that supplier travel, lodging, and meal costs conform to the supplier's published travel policy.
5. Determination of the reasonableness of airline travel, car rental, lodging, and meal costs.
6. Determination of the reasonableness of mileage allowance for using privately owned vehicles.
7. Determination of the reasonableness of supplier MIS costs.
8. Determination of the reasonableness of supplier consultant costs and verification that proposed consultants do not have a conflict of interest.
9. Determination of the reasonableness of supplier meeting and conference costs.
10. Determination that the supplier is consistent in classifying other direct costs and that the supplier is consistent in the procedures used to allocate other-direct costs to different jobs.
11. Determination whether all other direct cost expenses proposed by the supplier are necessary.
12. Determination of the adequacy of supplier-provided information in support of all other direct cost expenses.

The Reasonableness of Proposed Overhead and G & A Rates

If the service supplier is doing business with a governmental entity, the chances are that he or she will have been subjected to some sort of overhead rate audit by that government entity. Audit results are formalized into a rate agreement that tells the firm what rates will be used for prospective bidding purposes as well as for retrospective (close-out) purposes. The buyer should ask the service supplier for a copy of his or her latest governmental rate agreement. Failing that, the buyer should request that the service supplier divulge detailed estimates of the costs included in the overhead and G & A pool projections for the contract period in question, divulge estimated bases used in calculating rates for that period, and explain how the rates were derived. Failing that the buyer should request certified financial information that can be used to derive rate approximations.

The Reasonableness of Proposed Profit or Fee Rate

The buyer should assess the technical, management, and cost risk of the work as well as determine the degree to which the supplier is willing to assume that risk. Generally, higher cost estimates (padding of cost, either in quantity or rates) evidence an unwillingness by the supplier to assume risk. In addition to considering risk and the relative difficulty of the job, the buyer should consider the size of the job, the period of performance, the amount of investment being made by the supplier in performing the work, the amount of assistance (buyer-provided property and financing) the buying organization is providing, and the amount of subcontracting involved.

The final source-selection decision may be made without negotiation or further discussion, particularly in those situations where two or more proposals have been rated as "acceptable" and price competition is evident. In most procurements the buyer will make the source selection decision, giving full and due consideration to the technical/management team recommendations. In more complex procurements, the source-selection official may be a high-level manager in the organization, or even the general manager. If technical and/or price negotiations are considered necessary, a systematic approach must be taken to the negotiation process.

SUMMARY

Although price/cost should always be a factor in selecting a service supplier, it may not be the most important factor. A logical mix of technical/management and price/cost/business evaluation criteria may be more appropriate. The more technical the work, the more weight the technical criteria should be given.

Price/Cost Selection Criteria

The results of a price and/or cost analysis will be necessary when negotiating price with the supplier.

Price Analysis
Price analysis is the evaluation of a proposed price without examining either the separate cost elements or the level of profit that combine to yield the price.

Cost Analysis
Cost analysis is the evaluation of (a) the separate cost elements and proposed profit/fee of an offeror's cost or pricing data, and (b) the judgmental factors the offeror applied in projecting from that data to the estimated costs for supplying the service.

A Price May Be Justified Based on Price Analysis
1. Adequate price competition exists.
2. Price analysis alone clearly demonstrates that the proposed price is reasonable.

When Adequate Price Competition Exists
1. Two or more responsible offerors who are able to satisfy the solicitation requirements respond to the solicitation.
2. These offerors compete independently for a contract to be awarded to the responsible offeror submitting the lowest evaluated price.

The buyer should anticipate when price analysis alone will not be adequate and request cost data in the solicitation.

Nonprice Selection Criteria (Best-Value Source Selection)

When factors other than price/cost are considered in the proposal evaluation criteria and those criteria can be defined adequately, the organization often uses the following process:

1. An advance purchasing plan is developed.
2. A source selection plan is developed.
3. Offers are solicited using a written solicitation.
4. Technical/management and price/cost/business proposals are submitted.
5. Proposals are evaluated and scored.
6. A competitive range for negotiation is determined.
7. If two or more proposals are fully acceptable and price competition is present, the job is awarded and all offerors are notified.
8. If discussions are necessary, all offerors are notified of their status either inside or outside the competitive range.
9. Offerors within the competitive range are advised of any deficiencies in their proposals and invited to correct them.
10. After all of the requested proposal amendments have been made, offerors remaining within the competitive range are invited to submit BAFOs.
11. A final evaluation is made and an award is made.
12. The buyer notifies unsuccessful offerors, and briefs them upon request.

7

Negotiating and Awarding the Service Contract

If negotiations are necessary (normally expected when best-value source selection is used), they should be held with every offeror in the competitive range. The competitive range should include all those offerors whose proposals stand a reasonable chance of being selected for award. The range need not include all proposals, since some proposals may be so deficient that even substantive discussions will not correct them, in which case the buyer must be careful not to "level" or "cross-fertilize" one offeror's approach or method with another's. The buyer should, however, take pains to include several proposals within the competitive range: Service suppliers can readily find out that the buyer is negotiating on a sole-source basis and use that to advantage against the buyer.

STEPS IN THE NEGOTIATION PROCESS

Negotiation generally consists of seven steps, as listed in Table 7-1.
An explanation of each of the steps in the negotiation process follows.

TABLE 7-1   Steps in the negotiation process.

Planning/Preparation.
Organization.
Fact finding.
Setting negotiation objectives.
Prenegotiation review: Documenting the buyer's prenegotiation position as needed with cost/ price analysis, technical reports and the prenegotiation memorandum.
Negotiation conference.
Documenting the negotiation.

Planning/Preparation

Planning/preparation, the first step, is probably the most important. This step includes analyzing prices and costs as explained in chapter 6, developing a preliminary negotiation position(s) based on those analyses, and planning the strategy and tactics for the impending negotiation conference(s). The agenda for negotiation is a product of this step.

Organization

The second step includes organizing the buyer negotiation team and establishing the ground rules to be followed by the various members of the team. The buyer will generally want technical representatives and auditors or cost/price analysts to attend the more complex negotiation sessions.

Fact-Finding

The third step is conducting fact-finding. There are two major methods of fact-finding. The best method is to go over the proposal with the supplier team prior to the negotiation conference to understand their problems and approaches and learn what issues to explore in greater depth. Such preliminary discussions are not meant to end in any type of agreement: agreements should be reserved for the negotiation conference. The other major fact-finding method is to use the first part of the negotiation conference for fact-finding discussions with the supplier's negotiation team, essentially making the negotiation a two-stage affair.

Setting Negotiation Objectives

After gaining answers to initial questions in the fact-finding step and resolving those issues that can be easily resolved, the buyer team must identify those issues that remain unresolved and formulate positions on those issues. At this point the buyer should reevaluate the negotiation position developed in the planning step. At this stage it is best to formulate a range of positions, from the maximum price to the rock bottom price he or she could hope to pay, assuming everything went right in the negotiation. The price the buyer really expects to pay (the objective position) would be somewhere in the middle.

Prenegotiation Review

Most buyers need higher level approval for their negotiation positions. As a result the buyer must document the basis for his or her positions, including the price and/or cost analysis performed, in a prenegotiation review.

Documenting the Prenegotiation Position:
Price Analysis

The buyer should document the price analysis to prove that the purchase price is fair and reasonable. Such documentation should include the price the service supplier offered, the data used to evaluate the offer, the conclusions reached, and why the conclusions were sound.

Documenting the Prenegotiation Position:
Cost Analysis

If the buyer used technical reports written by engineers or other specialists to arrive at the cost position, those reports should be in the cost analysis documentation. These reports should cover findings that result from applying special technical knowledge to the elements of the proposal.

If auditor assistance was not requested, a cost/price analyst may be required to perform certain functions normally assigned to an auditor. The auditor or cost/price analyst report should include any financial effects of the proposed deal. The buyer should focus on any differences between technical and audit analyses (such as projections of direct labor hours). The auditor (if there is one involved in the action) should prepare a report after reviewing the facts as presented in the service supplier's books and records and evaluate the future costs projections. The auditor is not limited to those data submitted or identified in writing by the offeror. The auditor should comment on any cost data not submitted by the offeror that could have a significant effect on the negotiation position. Further, if the costs submitted are not accurate, current, or complete, the auditor should list and describe any inaccuracies or omissions in the audit report.

The designated cost/price analyst (or the buyer, if there is no assigned analyst) should collect and consolidate the several reports, adding comments and analyses as needed, in a format helpful to the buyer.

Documenting the Buyer's Position:
Prenegotiation Memoranda

Many organizations require their buyers to prepare prenegotiation memoranda, particularly for complex procurements. These memoranda generally include two elements: cost/profit analysis and attachments.

Prenegotiation Memorandum: Cost/Profit Analysis

This normally includes summary comparisons (spreadsheets reflecting the numbers) and an analysis of the information in those spreadsheets on a cost-element by cost-element basis (prose rationale for the numerical positions.)

Prenegotiation Memorandum: Attachments

This normally includes service supplier and subcontractor cost proposal(s); technical analyses of service supplier cost proposals; any available audit report(s); any appropriate technical specialist reports (including those of the cost/price analyst); and an explanation of both the profit/fee evaluation and the establishment of the prenegotiation position.

Negotiation Conference

In the negotiation conference, the buyer team brings to the table its planned strategy and tactics as well as its plan for achieving its cost and profit positions.

During the session, the buyer team must be prepared to employ (or to counter) common negotiation gambits and ploys. These include such things as making the other party appear unreasonable, putting the other party on the defensive, blaming some third party who is out of reach, the "sugar-vinegar" device, straw issues, the recess, the walkout, and the "here-it-is-Friday-afternoon-and-you've-got-a-plane-to-catch" squeeze. These tactics and other stratagems of negotiation are regularly employed (many times unknowingly) to arrive at mutually satisfactory agreements.

Negotiation Documentation

At the end of the negotiation conference(s) the buyer will want to document the negotiated agreement. Most organizations require that their buyers prepare negotiation memoranda, particularly for complex procurements. They further require that these memoranda be approved at some higher level of management.

The negotiation memorandum is the only document required after negotiations have been concluded. It tells the reader the story of the negotiations. What were the offered prices and the offeror's projected costs? What was the buyer's price objective and what were the costs supporting that goal? What cost data were submitted but not relied on (that is, not used)? What were the performance and contract type goals? What was discussed? What were the compelling arguments? What disposition was made of the principal points raised in preliminary analyses, included in the objective, and discussed in the negotiations? What values, costs and other factors support the agreed-upon price? If these are different from those supporting the objective, what justifications are there for the differences?

The negotiation memorandum is, first, a sales document that establishes the reasonableness of the agreement reached with the service supplier. Second, it is the permanent record of the buyer's decision. The negotiation memorandum relates all relevant specific details as it charts the progress of the procurement from proposal through negotiations to the final agreement. It will be the source document for reconstructing the events of the procurement, should that ever become necessary. The prudent buyer will construct the negotiation memorandum so that strangers can understand what happened and why.

To provide an adequate record, the negotiation memorandum must do several things. It must prove that the price is fair and reasonable, support the type of contract ultimately agreed upon, identify which cost data were relied upon and which were submitted by the service supplier but not relied upon. It should convince the reader that the buyer and his or her pricing team did all that needed to be and could be done to reach a fair and reasonable price.

The negotiation memorandum is written for the individual or group that determines whether the contract is approved. The audience should dictate the level of detail in the memorandum and, to some extent, its style. The buyer must strike a reasonable balance between too few words and too many.

The format of the negotiation memorandum will generally be spelled out in the organization's policy. Many organizations use a standard format similar to that discussed later on this chapter. However, the content of the negotiation memorandum must vary to report the actual events of the analysis and negotiation. The relevant events will vary depending on whether the negotiation is conducted to agree on the terms of a definitive contract, a definitive contract superseding a letter contract, new work added to an existing contract, or the final settlement of an incentive arrangement.

The most important part of the negotiation memorandum is the postnegotiation summary. This segment will include the cost/price analysis, the supplier's cost proposal, the buyer's negotiation objective, and the negotiation results tabulated in parallel form and broken down by major elements for cost and profit. The table of summary figures should be followed by a narrative explanation. Whether the summary figures will be for total contract value, total price of the major item, unit price for the major item, or some other presentation will depend on how the negotiations were conducted. The general rule is that the figures in the table should be presented in the form discussed in the negotiation. Since unit cost and profit figures may not give a true picture of the significance of each element, both total and unit values should appear in the narrative following the table. Finally, the buyer must award the contract.

AWARDING THE CONTRACT

Documenting Supplier Acceptance

With very few exceptions, the service contract should be a written document signed by both parties. It should contain all terms and conditions included in the specimen contract as well as any changes, modifications, and additions agreed to in the negotiations. Because it is generally signed by both parties, it is ordinarily a bilateral (two-party) contract.

Supplier acceptance can be effected on the face of the contract or by an acceptance similar to the following:

SUPPLIER ACCEPTANCE

This is a bilateral contract. The supplier must sign and return one copy of the contract to the buyer within _____ days to accept the contract. By signing the contract, the Supplier agrees to perform subject to the terms and conditions set forth herein.

_____   _____
Supplier Signature   Date

The buyer fills in the blank representing the number of days allowed for acceptance. Once signed and returned by the supplier, the contract becomes a binding bilateral contract.

The Award Process for Contracts Requiring Bonding

For those service contracts that have been bonded (typical for construction), the buyer will generally award the contract in two stages. In the first stage, the buyer will send an award notification to the supplier. This award notification will provide instructions to the supplier on submitting the performance and payment bonds and/or the insurance certificate as appropriate. The supplier will normally be given 10 to 15 days to submit the required documentation, which must then be reviewed and evaluated to ensure agreement with the terms of the solicitation and contract. A few days is normally adequate for this determination. Upon completing the necessary reviews, the formal contract is prepared for execution.

Some organizations use a combined solicitation and award document that facilitates the award process. For those organizations, the signed offer in the solicitation is accepted by the buyer on the same contract form, thus creating the bilateral contract between the two parties.

During the time between issuing the award notification and signing the formal contract, the contract is legally "voidable." If the supplier fails to return proper bonds or insurance, the contract may be voided. This is seldom done in practice because the supplier has a number of options for achieving compliance. Such options include changing sureties or obtaining individual sureties for the work.

Distributing Copies of the Signed Contract

Immediately after award, the buyer will need to distribute copies of the contract. Those organizations that employ the "original" and "duplicate original" system will need to retain the original and transmit the duplicate original to the supplier. Some organizations use a color coding system, with the original (retained by the buyer) on one color of paper, and the duplicate original (provided to the supplier) on a different color. Regardless of the system, the buyer's Accounting Department will need a signed copy of the contract for payment purposes. The service requestor and the quality assurance evaluator or inspector should also receive copies of the contract.

DEALING WITH UNSUCCESSFUL OFFERORS

After distribution, the buyer should return any bid bonds and provide notices of award to all unsuccessful offerors. Some organizations also publish their awards in the local media and/or on their bulletin boards. If an unsuccessful vendor requests an explanation of why it did not receive the award, a debriefing should be conducted in person or by phone. Normally, the explanation will be that the award was made to the lowest quoter. If this is not the case, the file should be clearly documented so that a good explanation may be given. The buyer should:

- Conduct the debriefing in a way that leaves no doubt that the award decision was made fairly, impartially, and objectively.
- Take care never to disclose any supplier's confidential business information (prices, wage rates, personnel, and so forth).
- Refrain from discussing the relative positions of the unsuccessful suppliers.

NOTICE TO PROCEED

Many service contracts do not really begin their term of performance until the buyer has issued the supplier a "notice to proceed." This notice is generally given after the buyer has briefed the supplier, and the supplier has obtained all necessary access and other clearances needed to begin the work. Construction contracts in particular often require special permits and approvals from governmental and other organizations before work can begin.

Notice to proceed should be given as soon after award as practicable. Many contracts with a project term (construction contracts for example) are written to require completion of the project within a certain number of days after receipt of the notice to proceed.

SUMMARY

Necessary negotiations should be held with every offeror in the competitive range; that is, with all offerors whose proposals stand a reasonable chance of being selected for award. Although the range need not include all proposals (some may be so deficient that even substantive discussions will not correct them), the buyer should take pains to undertake negotiations with several offerors.

Negotiation generally consists of seven steps:

1. *Planning/preparation*—price and cost analysis, developing prenegotiation position(s), and strategy and tactics.
2. *Organization*—choosing the negotiation team and assigning tasks, rights, and responsibilities.
3. *Fact-finding*—preliminary discussions not meant to end in any type of agreement, held in order to understand the potential suppliers problems and approaches, and learn what issues to explore in greater depth.
4. *Setting negotiation objectives*—reevaluating the prenegotiation position considering information gathered in fact-finding. It is best to formulate a range of positions reaching from best- to worst-case.
5. *Prenegotiation review*—documenting the buyer's negotiation position. Most buyers need higher level approval for their negotiation positions. Documentation should include the price analysis, the cost analysis (if any), and any technical reports used in arriving at the cost position.

   Many organizations require that the prenegotiation position be documented in a specific format called a prenegotiation memorandum. These memoranda generally include two elements: cost/profit analysis and attachments. The cost/profit analysis is a spreadsheet of costs and a verbal explanation of the cost positions taken. Attachments include supplier and subcontractor cost proposal(s), technical analyses of those proposals, any available audit report(s), appropriate technical specialist reports, and explanations of both the profit/fee evaluation and of how the prenegotiation position for profit/fee was established.

6. *Negotiation conference*—the negotiation team uses the negotiation positions, strategy, and tactics previously developed to negotiate an agreement favorable to both parties.
7. *Negotiation documentation*—the negotiation memorandum, the only postnegotiation documentation required, tells the story of the negotiations so that higher levels of management may evaluate the deal. Many companies have a standard format. The buyer should include everything that happened in the negotiation plus whatever explanations are necessary to convince the reviewers that the deal was a good one.

In most instances a service contract should be bilateral: The supplier should sign a copy and return it to the buying organization. For service contracts that require bonding and/or insurance, award is generally a two-stage process in which notification of award is followed by a short period (10–15 days) in which the supplier is expected to secure adequate bonding and/or insurance. The formal contract is signed by both parties only after the supplier's proof of bonding or insurance has been determined to be in compliance with contract terms and conditions. If the supplier fails to secure adequate bonding or insurance within the above period, the contract may be voided.

After contract award is final, copies of the contract must be distributed to the supplier, the buying organization's Accounting Department, the service requestor, and the quality assurance inspector.

Unsuccessful offerors must be notified of contract award. A briefing should be given to any unsuccessful offeror asking to know the rationale behind the award choice. The briefing should concentrate on explaining why the award decision was fair and impartial, and care must be taken to avoid divulging confidential information about other offerors (their expenses, wage rates, and offers for example).

Often the contract term of performance does not really begin until the buying organization has issued the supplier a notice to proceed. Although such notice should be issued as soon as reasonably practicable, it should not be issued until the supplier has procured all permits, clearances, and licenses necessary to do the work.

8

Service Contract Administration

The term "contract administration" means any activity taken by either the buyer or the supplier during the time from contract award to contract closeout. Table 8-1 contains a list of objectives that the buyer administering the contract attempts to achieve.

ROUTINE VERSUS NONROUTINE CONTRACT ADMINISTRATION

The buyer's purpose in service contract administration is to assure compliance with the terms and conditions of the contract. All service contracts require certain contract administration steps regardless of their nature, complexity, or dollar value. These steps include work control; assuring compliance with contract terms and conditions; assuring adequate financial control of the contract; and monitoring, auditing, and approving supplier systems. These actions are sometimes referred to as "routine" contract administration.

The extent to which any contract will require nonroutine contract administration cannot be predicted and will depend on certain factors, including the complexity of the required services and the riskiness of contract performance. The specific actions to be taken cannot be planned in advance.

The authors wish to acknowledge Educational Services Institute, Arlington, Virginia for its permission to adapt selected sections of the U.S. Postal Service Contract Administration Reference Guide (1987). Pages 1A-1 and 2; 2A-1, 2, 5, and 6; 2D-1 to 2D-7; 2D-13 to 2D-16; 3A-1 to 3A-3; and 3B-1 to 3B-10 from the Guide, as adapted to service contract administration, are found in the following chapter.

TABLE 8-1   Objectives of contract administration.

Assuring both buyer and supplier performance comply with the contract.
Achieving prompt and fair resolution of any problems that arise during performance.
Negotiating modifications to the contract, to include any necessary adjustments in cost or
  schedule or both.
Assuring smooth flow of work to the supplier.
Assuring expeditious handling of invoices and payments.
Accomplishing all necessary administrative actions.

THE CONTRACT ADMINISTRATION TEAM

The need for teamwork between the assigned buyer and the user/requesting office does not end when the contract is awarded. The need for teamwork may actually intensify during contract administration.

The buyer responsible for administering a service contract must be ever mindful that he or she is the organization's "agent" for purposes of administering the contract. As the organization's specific, limited agent for contract administration, the buyer is ultimately responsible for all contract performance matters. However, the buyer rarely has the broad expertise needed to assure successful contract completion and will generally need to delegate some contract administration duties to other members of the contract administration team.

A diagram of a typical contract administration team is shown in Appendix H. An explanation of the duties of different team members follows.

Buyer Responsibilities

The buyer is responsible for the legal, contract, and business relationship between his or her organization and the service supplier. The buyer is responsible for interpreting contract terms and conditions and for analyzing performance costs. Based on input from other members of the contract administration team, the buyer is responsible for issuing changes and negotiating modifications to the contract. As leader and manager of the contract administration team the buyer must plan, organize, coordinate, direct, and control the activities of team members. The success or failure of the team is largely due to the managerial and leadership abilities of the buyer.

Responsibilities of the Buyer's Representative

For some contracts, the buyer may find it advisable to designate a person to act, within certain limitations, as his or her representative in administering a contract. The buyer's representative will usually be a person from the user/requesting office or someone with expertise in the area of the contract effort who possesses the necessary background to administer the contract. The buyer's representative's primary tasks are monitoring performance, evaluating work as it progresses, and recommending final acceptance of completed work.

A buyer's representative should always be appointed in writing. The appointing document must clearly define the scope and limitations of the assigned authority. The supplier should be given a copy of the appointment letter.

Changes in the authority of (as well as the termination of) a buyer's representative must also be made in writing. When the appointment covers more than one contract, each contract should have its own appointment letter.

A buyer's representative may be given the following responsibilities. The tasks listed will not all be applicable to every contract. Not all tasks must be delegated to the representative.

1. Review the statement of work and buyer quality assurance plan to assure the work required is understood.
2. Assist the user/requesting office personnel in development of estimates needed for change orders/modifications, for the exercise of term options, and to adjust wage rates during contract performance.
3. Assist the buyer in conducting preproposal conferences, prestart conferences, and supplier site visits, as necessary.
4. Assist the buyer as requested in negotiating change orders and modifications and negotiating contract option years.
5. Assist the buyer in general administration of the contract.
6. Monitor the service supplier's performance through inspection, and notify the supplier of deficiencies observed.
7. Record and report to the buyer any incidents of faulty or nonconforming work, delays, or problems.
8. Submit a monthly report of service performance rendered in support of the contract.
9. Assure that the supplier abides by all the required provisions of the FLSA, CWHSSA, SCA, and/or Davis-Bacon and related acts, as applicable.
10. Make recommendations to the buyer regarding payments, retention, and deductions from payments.
11. Make recommendations to the buyer regarding issuance of contract discrepancy reports, cure notices, and show cause notices.
12. Supervise any assigned quality assurance evaluators or inspectors in the performing their duties. Assure they properly implement the buyer's quality assurance plan and that they conduct regular QA meetings with the service supplier.

13. In accordance with buyer-provided appointment letter instructions, issue work orders (sometimes called task or delivery orders) under the terms of assigned indefinite-delivery (blanket order) type contracts.
14. Maintain working files and records.
15. Approve supplier material and equipment submittals, if required.
16. Review and approve quality assurance surveillance plans submitted by assigned quality assurance evaluators/inspectors.
17. Provide the buyer with any supplier-requested change, deviation, or waiver requests. Provide a recommendation on each such request, supported with appropriate documentation.
18. Provide the buyer with recommendations regarding changes or revisions to statements of work and quality assurance plans that will lead to improvements on the current and/or future contracts.
19. Assist the buyer in administering health and safety laws and regulations as they relate to the work sites.

Limitations on the Buyer's Representative's Authority

The buyer's representative is not generally given authority to deviate from the contract statement of work. In addition, the representative is rarely given authority to direct or interfere with methods of performance by the service supplier or to issue instructions directly to any supplier personnel, unless the methods being used constitute an immediate safety hazard. Buyer's representatives are almost never permitted to award, agree to, or execute a contract or contract modification, or to obligate the buying organization in any way for the payment of money. With few exceptions, the representative is prohibited from making a final decision on any matter that would be subject to appeal under the Disputes provisions (mediation, arbitration, or litigation) of the contract. Lastly, representatives are rarely permitted to terminate a contract either for the buyer's convenience or because of the supplier's default/cause.

For a number of reasons, the buyer may determine that it is in the best interest of the firm for the buyer's representative to have limited authority to issue emergency changes in amounts not exceeding a set dollar limit. This type of delegation of authority may be necessary to avoid delaying changes which must be implemented immediately in order to protect against the loss of property or preclude a work stoppage.

Responsibilities of the Quality Assurance Evaluator/Inspector (QAE)

If a project QAE or inspector is appointed, such appointments should always be written. The appointment should clearly define the scope of the inspection task and the limits of the inspector's authority. Any changes in (or termination of) the project QAE/inspector's authority should also be made in writing.

A QAE/inspector should report directly to the buyer's representative if one exists and may act for the representative in many matters. The inspector's most important tasks include:

1. Accomplishing surveillance required by the buyer's quality assurance plans and schedules.
2. Completing and submitting to the buyer's representative inspection reports as required in the contract's quality assurance plans.
3. Certifying satisfactorily completed work, payment deductions, and other administrative actions or poor or non-performed work.
4. Assisting the buyer's representative in identifying necessary changes to the contract, preparing in-house estimates, conducting quality assurance meetings, approving supplier submittals, and maintaining working files.
5. Promptly furnishing the buyer's representative with any requests for supplier-requested changes, deviations, or waivers.
6. Making recommendations to the buyer's representative regarding changes or revisions to the statement of work or quality assurance plans that will lead to improvements either on the current contract or on future contracts.

Limitations on the QAE/Inspector's Authority

A QAE/inspector should *generally not* be permitted to allow deviations from contract requirements, direct or interfere with the methods of performance by the service supplier, or issue instructions directly to any service-supplier personnel unless the methods being used present an immediate safety hazard. In addition, the QAE/inspector is generally not permitted to issue any instructions that would constitute a contractual change. The limitations imposed on the buyer's representative are similarly imposed on the QAE/inspector.

Other Contract Administration Team Members

Depending on the complexity of the contract, other people may also become involved in contract administration. These personnel will provide their input as required by the buyer or the buyer's representative. (See the contract administration team diagram in Appendix H.)

PLANNING FOR CONTRACT ADMINISTRATION

In its manual created for the U.S. Postal Service (1987), Educational Services Institute advocates a contract administration plan. As the person with overall responsibility for orchestrating the contract administration team effort, the buyer should prepare a separate management plan for each contract. The plans should be prepared at the time the contract is awarded.

The Contract Administration Plan Outline

The central element of the plan will be an outline of all specific tasks that both the supplier and buyer can be expected to perform under the contract. The plan should assign responsibility for the tasks identified and spell out procedures for coordinating, communicating, and controlling the contract. The outline should answer the following questions:

1. What deliverables, if any, must the supplier provide?
2. What tasks must be performed?
3. What data must be generated?
4. What information must be provided by the buyer to the supplier and vice versa?
5. Where will contract activities be performed and where will they be inspected?
6. What is the sequence of contract activities and what is the schedule for those activities?
7. How will the supplier perform the contract?
8. Who will accomplish each of the contract administration tasks?

The plan should encompass each stage in the contract administration process as described in Table 8-2.

The plan developed by the contract administration team should be like a flexible budget; it should change as work progresses. It needs to be flexible enough to permit reallocation of team responsibilities or addition of tasks that could not be anticipated at the time of award. The contract administration plan should be prepared when a requisition is received, and updated periodically as necessary.

TABLE 8-2   Contract administration stages: Issues in the plan outline.

Planning and organizing for contract administration.
Coordinating and monitoring supplier performance.
Receipt, inspection, and acceptance of services.
Receiving invoices and making payments.
Contract closure: Directing/controlling supplier activities needed to close out the contract.

ORDERING AND WORK AUTHORIZATION

Under some types of service contracts, ordering and work authorization are deferred until after award. Examples of such contracts are indefinite-delivery type contracts, time-and-material/labor-hour contracts, and cost-reimbursement type contracts. In such cases, ordering becomes a postaward or contract administration matter.

Indefinite-Delivery Type Contracts

Work ordering processes under indefinite-delivery type contracts and time-and-materials/labor-hour contracts are generally quite similar. The service or item user completes a standard work order or delivery order form in which the line item description of the desired service(s) is copied directly from the contract and the unit price is copied directly from the contract schedule. The desired quantity is multiplied times the unit price to arrive at a total. This work/delivery order is generally routed to either a buyer's representative or buyer for signature and copies are then distributed to the supplier, the customer activity, and the finance office.

Work completion, work inspection and acceptance, invoicing, and payment under an indefinite-delivery type contract follow normal procedures. A flow diagram for a typical ordering and payment cycle is shown in Appendix I.

Time-and-Materials Contracts

The process for time-and-material/labor-hour contracts differs in that the work/delivery order prepared by the service user is generally accompanied by a brief statement of work and an in-house estimate for work. Many organizations then request a formal cost proposal from the supplier. The cost proposal then forms the basis for negotiation and agreement on a firm-fixed-price for the work order. Other organizations issue the work order without agreement on a firm-fixed-price and permit the supplier to bill actual hours expended. Rates applied would, of course, be those agreed upon in the basic contract.

Cost-Reimbursement Contracts

Cost-reimbursement contract work control procedures are often considerably more complex. The following process, comprised of annual work plans, work authorizations and notices to proceed (NTPs) can be used to assist in cost and schedule control in large-dollar value cost-reimbursement contracts extending over several years.

The Annual Work Plan

The annual work plan (AWP) is central to the total process because it provides the initial definition of tasks to be performed in the budget year and a schedule for accomplishment. The AWP provides for a balance of funding guidance and program schedule requirements. During the AWP review, the supplier resource projections are approved and the tasks to be undertaken are scheduled.

Creating the Annual Work Plan (AWP)

Preparing the AWP will generally begin in the fourth quarter of the fiscal year preceding the budget year. The supplier creates the AWP using funding information, information on scope of the desired project and milestones from the current master production schedule provided by the buyer. The required funding information consists of expected funding levels for the ensuing (budgeted) fiscal year and for subsequent years. The supplier will submit a draft AWP to the buyer's representative prior to the beginning of the new budget year. The supplier and the buyer's representative will adjust the AWP following receipt of final budget guidance and prepare to implement the AWP at the beginning of the new fiscal year.

Elements of the AWP

The specific elements of an AWP generally include goals and assumptions; work authorization review results; and a schedule, staffing plan, and cost estimate for the budget year. The AWP should be updated as needed during the fiscal year.

Work Authorizations

Work authorizations are integral to the financial flow associated with the contract. They generally contain a scope of work complete with work breakdown structure, the duration of the work authorization, the baseline cost estimate for the work, and a list of the milestones remaining to work completion with their accompanying NTPs referenced to the existing AWP. The following points characterize the work authorization procedure as it exists in many organizations:

1. The work authorization is a contractual (fund obligating) instrument, whose establishment and change require contract modification.
2. The cost estimate associated with a work authorization is the baseline cost for the work covered by the authorization.

3. Funds obligated to the contract will be allotted to work units by appropriate work authorizations. Such allotments will be followed (triggered) by NTPs for specific tasks. When performance of a task extends over multiple fiscal years, incremental funding will generally be employed.
4. The cumulative funding allotment for all work authorizations up to a given date is evaluated with respect to the contract's limitation of funds provisions. The supplier should provide the buyer with an estimate of the funds required to continue performance and notify the buyer if the accumulated costs are expected to exceed 75 percent of the total allotted funding within the next 60 days.

Notice to Proceed (NTP)
The supplier is issued an NTP when it is time to begin each new work unit. A work authorization allowing payment for the work unit should be sent to the buying organization's Accounting Department at the same time. The AWP controls the sequence of work units for which NTPs and work authorizations are issued.

The Effect of Changes on Cost-Reimbursement
Ordering
Changes to various features of the work are inevitable. If changes in the work result in changes in the baseline cost of the contract, the work authorizations should be modified accordingly. Usually changes involving ongoing work have the largest dollar impact and require prompt action to avoid delaying completion milestones. Ordinarily the supplier will designate a portion of the budget as contingency and will respond to small changes in the work by using the contingency fund. When the estimated value of the change exceeds available contingency, the supplier will provide written justification for revising the work authorization to cover the change, including an allowance for additional contingency.

If changes arise that are outside the cost estimate, schedule, and/or scope documented in the work authorization, the supplier should prepare a program-level estimate of the cost and schedule impacts of such proposed changes in sufficient detail to support the formal change process. If the change is approved, the buyer's representative revises the appropriate work authorization (including requirements documentation) and allots the necessary funding to cover estimated additional costs.

All modifications to work authorizations require a modification to the contract.

NEGOTIATING CHANGES TO CONTRACTS

Ideally, a contract should contain all provisions necessary for completing the work and discharging both parties' obligations. In practice, however, few contracts are complete without some type of modification. Some modifications are simply administrative changes that do not affect the substance of the contract. Others involve substantial changes to the price, quantity, quality, delivery, or other terms originally agreed to by the buyer and the supplier.

The buyer's authority under any given contract is defined by the contract's provisions. Those provisions should provide means to alter the contract after award. They should permit the parties to equitably alter the delivery schedule or the price to be paid in correspondence with other changes in the contract's terms. The contract must give the buyer the authority to make such changes. It should also allow the supplier or the buyer "relief" if the other party does not perform as originally agreed.

Definitions
The following terms are used in connection with contract changes during administration:

Administrative Change   This is a change that does not affect the substantive rights of the parties to the contract. Changing the paying office or the cost accounting code would be administrative changes. Administrative changes may be made unilaterally.

Cardinal Change   This is a change outside the scope of the contract. Cardinal changes alter some essential element of the work such as the quantity of services to be ordered. Cardinal changes are not authorized under most changes provisions. If a buyer or other contract administration team member orders a cardinal change and the supplier performs it, the supplier will be entitled to an equitable adjustment in price and/or schedule, and the buyer may be found to have committed a legal breach of the contract.

Change Order   This is a written order, signed by the buyer, directing the supplier to implement a change authorized in the changes provision in the contract. As the supplier has already agreed to make any changes listed in the changes provision, change orders can be issued unilaterally. They can be issued for several reasons, including a change in the work required, a change in user needs, and factors beyond the control of either the buyer or the service supplier.

Constructive Change   A constructive change is one that a supplier acts upon or is impacted by even though the buyer had no intention of issuing a formal change. For example, the supplier's delivery schedule is changed when buyer-provided property is provided later than contractually promised.

Contract Modification   This is a written alteration in the work, place of performance, delivery date, contract period, price, quantity, or any other contract provision. There are two major types of contract modifications.

Unilateral Modification   A unilateral modification is a contract modification that is signed only by the buyer. As previously noted, administrative changes and changes authorized by a changes provision may be made unilaterally. Changes authorized by other contract provisions (including notices of contract termination in accordance with either the termination for convenience or termination for default/cause provision) may also be made unilaterally.

Bilateral Modification   A bilateral modification is a contract modification signed by both the buyer and the supplier and implemented by mutual agreement. Bilateral modifications are generally used to modify the substantive terms of the contract. They are also used to make negotiated equitable adjustments resulting from the issuance of an unpriced change order and to definitize letter contracts.

Supplemental Agreement   A supplemental agreement is a form of bilateral modification. An equitable adjustment negotiated following a change order is a typical supplemental agreement.

The following discussion will further explain a typical changes provision for a service contract, policy and procedure for invoking change orders and constructive changes, and the use of supplemental agreements in making bilateral modifications and equitable adjustments.

A Typical Service Changes Provision

Every contract should contain a changes provision. Such provisions are invoked frequently; they cover not only changes directed in writing by the buyer but also constructive changes, which are changes caused, possibly inadvertently, by the actions or inactions of a member of the contract administration team. The following changes provision (shown broken into sections covering change authorization, equitable adjustment, supplier claims and disputes) is typical of the type included in service contracts.

Change Authorization

The buyer may at any time, by a written order, and without notice to the sureties, if any, make changes, within the general scope of this contract, in any one or more of the following:
(i) description of services to be performed;

(ii) time of performance (i.e., hours of the day, days of the week, etc.);
and
(iii) place of performance of the services.

Several key phrases are used in the first sentence:

"The Buyer May..."
The provision restricts the authority to make a change to the buyer. Occasionally the buyer's authorized representative is included. The service supplier should be alerted to the fact that not every person on the contract administration team is authorized to direct changes. If an individual without authority directs a change and the supplier acts on that direction, the buyer may be held to that change under the doctrine of constructive change.

"At Any Time"
The timing of a change can have a financial impact on a service supplier and therefore require a price adjustment.

"By Written Order"
A written change order must be issued. Oral changes are sometimes recognized under the rationale that ratification of those changes was only fair to the service supplier. The service supplier that carries out an orally directed change on the assumption that it will be ratified in writing later, however, does so at its own risk.

"Without Notice to the Sureties"
A surety is an individual or corporation (often an insurance company) that is legally liable for the debt, default, or failure of the supplier to fulfill its contractual obligations. This phrase says that the buyer has the right to change the contract without notifying the sureties and without getting their written agreement. The surety's obligation therefore remains unchanged.

"Within the General Scope"
Controversies over what is or is not within the general scope of a contract have generated many legal fights, none of which has conclusively defined the term. The scope of a contract is "what should be regarded as fairly and reasonably within the contemplation of the parties when the contract was agreed to." If work ordered by a change is within the scope of the contract, it is binding on the service supplier; if it is not within that scope, however, it is extra work that the service supplier can legally decline to perform. The term has been interpreted broadly to give the buyer flexibility. The buyer must determine what lies within the general scope on a case-by-case basis,

often through negotiations with the service supplier. In the public sector the difficulty of determining whether a given change is within the scope of the original contract is compounded by the issue of whether the buyer can order the change without justifying it as a sole-source purchase. To avoid this conundrum, buyers often interpret the contract's scope narrowly.

"In Any of the Following..."
The provision permits unilateral changes in description of services, as well as in time and place of performance. The buyer is generally given wide legal latitude to make changes covering a broad range of issues.

Equitable Adjustment

> If any such change causes an increase or decrease in the cost of, or the time re-
> quired for, the performance of any part of the work under this contract,
> whether changed or not changed by any such order, an equitable adjustment
> shall be made in the contract price or delivery schedule, or both, and the con-
> tract shall be modified in writing accordingly.

If the change ordered by the buyer increases or decreases the contract price or the time needed for performance, the buyer is obligated to afford the supplier an adjustment of either the contract price or the performance schedule or both.

Buyers are cautioned to heed the fact that the supplier may still be due an equitable adjustment in price and/or schedule due to changes in some other unchanged work even if the aspect of the work being changed does not experience an increase or decrease in price or time needed for performance. This is a "ripple effect."

Supplier Claims

> Any claim by the supplier for adjustment under this provision must be asserted
> within 30 days from the date of receipt by the supplier of the notification of
> change: *Provided, however,* that the buyer, if he decides that the facts justify
> such action, may receive and act upon any such claim asserted at any time prior
> to final payment under this contract. Where the cost of property made obsolete
> or excess as a result of a change is included in the supplier's claim for adjust-
> ment, the buyer shall have the right to prescribe the manner of disposition of
> such property.

Although the supplier is generally obliged to submit a request for equita-ble adjustment within 30 days, the buyer is permitted to accept and act on claims submitted after the 30-day suspense date for the claim for equitable adjustment. Prompt action would be the preferred option because it benefits both the buyer and the service supplier.

Disputes

> Failure to agree to any adjustment shall be a dispute concerning a question of fact within the meaning of the provision of this contract entitled *Disputes*. However, nothing in this provision shall excuse the supplier from proceeding with the contract as changed.

The buyer must be aware that every change order and every contract modification can potentially result in a dispute subject to the disputes provision of the contract. Disputes normally arise when the buyer and supplier cannot agree on the amount of the "equitable adjustment" in price and/or schedule.

The last sentence is often considered the most important one in the provision. It gives the service supplier the "duty to proceed" with the work as changed even though he or she may not want to and otherwise believes the change is neither in his or her interest or in the interest of the buyer. This part of the provision is also important in that if there is no agreement on a price or schedule adjustment when the change order is issued, the service supplier must go on working and try to negotiate an equitable adjustment later. If the supplier walks off the job, he or she risks the possibility of a termination of the contract for default/cause.

Constructive Changes

Although the typical changes provision states that the buyer must make all changes in writing, there have been many cases in which oral directions by the buyer and others have been held to have been legitimately ordered changes. Such changes occur quite frequently in construction and other service contracting.

Buyer actions (or failures to act) that are construed by the supplier to have been ordered unilaterally by the buying organization (even though they do not fit the formal requirements for change orders) are called constructive changes. Any conduct of a buyer or buyer's representative requiring a supplier to perform work not required by the contract can, in the right circumstances, be deemed a constructive change.

Types/Origins of Constructive Changes
Constructive changes can be classified by their origins as follows:

Interpretations by Buyer's Representatives or QAE/Inspectors
Even individuals who do not have official authority to change a contract can, by their actions or by their interpretation of the statement of work, still alter the service contract. There is often a fine line between what is technical monitoring and what is directing a change. A court of law may determine that a certain buyer direction is a *de facto* change order and grant the supplier administrative relief for the additional cost of the work. The legal doctrine of constructive change complicates administration of contract changes because it is hard for the buyer to know in every case what actions are being taken by buyer representatives and QAE/inspection personnel.

Error in Interpreting the Statement of Work
Buyer personnel should be particularly careful about the manner with which they administer the service changes provision. Problems can arise whenever the supplier makes continual requests for interpretation of the work statement and guidance on work methods. The interpretations or decisions made by the buyer and/or buyer's representative can lead to supplier claims. If a buyer with authority to make changes misinterprets the requirements of the statement of work, a court may be required to determine that the error is a constructive change. This is particularly prevalent where the statement of work permits the service supplier freedom to choose between various work methods, and the buyer insists after award that the supplier use method A instead of a less expensive alternative. Courts of law hesitate to side with the buyer merely because the change was not put into writing.

The constructive change doctrine also applies in situations where the contract contains a performance work statement and the buyer or buyer's representative insists on a different standard of performance. If the buyer's interpretation of the work statement requires more work than the supplier expected or included in bid calculations, the supplier is due an equitable adjustment.

Failure to Correct a Defective Work Statement
Failure to issue a change order to correct a defective statement of work is basis for declaring that a constructive change had been made. Since the buyer should have issued a change order but did not, the supplier should be compensated for the buying organization's error and also should be permitted some relief for the additional work and wasted effort caused by the defective work statement.

Changes Outside the Scope

A buyer may issue a written change order for work that is later found to be outside the general scope of the contract. For example, although a changes provision generally allows for unilateral orders altering the place of performance, a substantial change in place of performance under certain types of contracts may be outside the scope.

Acceleration

Orders to speed up performance or to perform by some date earlier than that required in the contract are referred to as acceleration. The buyer can accelerate contract performance by adding performance requirements while failing to extend the completion date in proportion to the additional work required. Since the buyer is ordering more work in the same performance period, the extra cost to the supplier is the difference in cost between performance "as originally estimated" and performance "as modified due to acceleration." Acceleration claims are very common in construction service contracting. Buyers must be very certain they know what supplier delays are considered excusable under the contract's "excusable delay" or "force majeure" provision. If the buyer requires the service supplier to perform on time even though the supplier is permitted an excusable delay, the buyer can be found to have accelerated the contract.

Changes in the Quantity of Work

Very few changes provisions permit changes to be made in the quantity of work. Such changes are invariably outside the scope of the contract. In the federal government, additional work is often considered new procurement and subject to requirements for obtaining competition. The buyer should generally consider substantial reductions in or deletions from the work as actually partial terminations rather than changes. Even if the addition or deletion of work is defined as an alteration in the statement of work, it will often not be authorized by the service contract changes provision.

Failure to Cooperate

The buyer and other personnel on the contract administration team have an implied duty to cooperate with the supplier. This duty includes furnishing buyer property on time and in the condition promised, as well as refraining from actions that would hinder the supplier's progress. If buyer action requires the supplier to alter the work phasing or schedule, it will probably be construed as a constructive change. If the buyer can be found to have not lived up to the contract or to have hindered the supplier, the supplier will generally be eligible for an equitable adjustment.

Supplemental Agreements

Supplemental agreements are used to finalize change orders and make changes beyond the scope of the contract. They accomplish any and all of the following purposes listed in Table 8-3.

If a supplemental agreement materially decreases the supplier's obligations, the buyer's organization should obtain additional consideration. Examples of such consideration include reduction in price, and faster or earlier work performance.

Supplemental Agreements in Change Order Finalization

Whenever feasible, the buyer should attempt to negotiate a change by supplemental agreement, rather than by issuing a "two-part change order" (a unilateral change order followed by negotiation of an equitable adjustment in price). This approach is generally preferred for several reasons. It places the buyer in a better bargaining position, permits the buyer to negotiate the change as well as the plans for making the change, reduces the probability of the supplier making a claim due to a constructive change, and decreases the administrative burden of the entire process.

Supplemental Agreements for Changes Outside the Scope

As discussed earlier, changes made pursuant to a typical changes provision must be within the general scope of the contract. When an anticipated modification is beyond the scope of the contract, it should be made by supplemental agreement.

A modification should be deemed beyond the scope of the contract if one or more of the circumstances detailed in Table 8-4 is present.

TABLE 8-3   Purposes of supplemental agreements.

Finalize equitable adjustments:

1. Of price and/or schedule agreed on after issuance of a change order under the changes provision;
2. Required in connection with contract provisions other than the changes provision.

Formalize a claim made in a termination for convenience.
Formalize decisions rendered by a court.
Allow a supplier to complete a contract after nonexcusable delay.
Effect changes that are out of scope of the contract.

TABLE 8-4   Characteristics of modifications beyond the contract scope.

The nature of the work under the modification is materially different from that covered by the original contract.

The quantities of work called for under the modification are substantially greater than those covered by the original contract.

The time required for performing the modification significantly increases the overall performance time.

The contract environment and/or risk of performance have been significantly changed.

As a general rule both private- and public-sector buyers should avoid adding work by supplemental agreement when it is possible to obtain the work under a new, competitively awarded contract.

Negotiating and Implementing Supplemental Agreements

The following steps should be taken to arrive at and implement supplemental agreements.

1. *Get an independent in-house estimate*: An independent estimate (based on the changed work statement) should be prepared when the buying organization determines there is a need for a supplemental agreement. This estimate should be prepared before receipt of the supplier's proposal.
2. *Prepare a request for modification proposal*: The formal solicitation must perform the functions listed in Table 8-5.
3. *Investigate the availability of funding*: The buyer should get an affirmative, written declaration from the Accounting Department that funds will be made available, so that the supplemental agreement can be executed. The buyer should not release a solicitation without funds.
4. *Perform analysis and negotiations*: Proposal analysis and negotiations should be conducted in accordance with organization policy. As these are sole-source negotiations, considerable attention must be given to the use

TABLE 8-5   Functions of a formal solicitation (supplemental agreement).

Provide a statement of work covering the changed work.

Clarify which parts of the original contract are applicable to the changed work.

Include:
  Cost proposal requirements;
  Performance schedule;
  Receipt, inspection and acceptance requirements.

Provide, if possible, for a firm-fixed-price quotation.

of cost analysis (in addition to price analysis and profit analysis) to arrive at a negotiation position with the supplier. Also, if the supplemental agreement will make any material change (that is, a change outside the scope of the changes provision) in a construction contract, the buyer must generally require the consent of the surety holding the performance and payment bonds.

5. *Document the agreement*: The buyer should document the supplemental agreement in order to promote effective and efficient contract administration. Documentation must be complete and correct.

The buyer should establish a separate file for each change. The file should generally include the proposed change request document, the contract change documents, the buyer's request for modification proposal, the supplier's proposal, the buyer's proposal analysis, the memorandum of negotiations, the in-house estimate of the cost of the changed work, the buyer's determination that a change is necessary, and a change order form completed and signed by both the supplier and the buyer.

EXERCISING RENEWAL OPTIONS IN SERVICE CONTRACTS

Renewal options are contract extensions provided for in the original contract. They are exercised at the unilateral discretion of the buyer and provide the buyer with the ability to continue using the services of satisfactory suppliers for additional periods of time. Exercising options costs less than new solicitations for the same services. Since option provisions are contained in the original contract, the buyer must decide to exercise the option before the original contract expires. Although exercising options creates a modification to the contract, the option exercise process and the logic behind it are sufficiently different to warrant a separate discussion.

Including Option Provisions in the Contract

The decision to include options (generally term options in service contracts) in a contract must be made when the solicitation package is developed. If the contract is to contain option(s) the solicitation must advise potential bidders of that fact, and a similar option provision entitled "Option to Extend The Term of the Contract" must be included in the specimen contract. The option provision generally gives the buyer the right to extend the contract under the same terms and conditions as those originally negotiated for two to four additional one-year periods. Since the basic term without options is one year for most service contracts, the resulting total term is often for three to five years. Although a typical option provision defines both the initial term and each option renewal period as being one year in length, there is nothing preventing shorter terms.

The Decision to Exercise

Decision Criteria
The quality of service-supplier performance is the most pertinent factor in considering whether to exercise an option to extend the contract. Reasonableness of price in relation to the current market conditions is also important.

Timing
If the buyer determines not to exercise the option, he or she should send a letter to the service supplier at least 60 days prior to the contract expiration date stating intent not to exercise the option. If the buyer decides to exercise the option, he or she should send the service supplier a preliminary notice of intent to renew. This is an important point. The typical option provision states that the supplier must have 60-days notice. If the option provision contains the usual notice requirement, the supplier has the contractual right to refuse the option exercise if notified on or after the 59th day prior to contract expiration. Presenting the supplier with notice of intent to exercise the option will generally not commit the buyer to actually exercise the option. However, if the buyer's full intention is to exercise, notice must not reach the supplier late.

Although it is not a good business practice to do so, the buyer will generally have the legal right not to exercise an option even after notice of intent to exercise. The buyer is obligated, however, to give the service supplier as much advance notice of the change of intent as possible.

Setting a Price for the Extended Service Period
The price of retaining the supplier's services for additional option periods should be apparent from reading the contract. Some buyers prefer to pre–price options by including a separate line item in the original contract for each year's performance. This pricing structure permits price adjustments to accommodate only those changes (if any) necessitated by the FLSA.

Other buyers prefer to fix only the price for the first year's requirements, including an economic price adjustment provision in the contract which will adjust the price of later option periods based on an index of some kind. The normal procedure for making adjustments in the price of services from one contract period to the next (option) period is to request a cost proposal, evaluate it, and negotiate the new prices with the service supplier. Price negotiations in this context are generally somewhat perfunctory unless the economic price adjustment provision or other provision governing the process has been poorly drafted. It is generally not a good practice to fix the price only for the first year and provide for year-end price negotiations to establish the following year's prices.

Buyers working in the public sector have the additional problem of adjusting rates to accommodate changes in the SCA. Those interested in the procedures for accomplishing this should contact the authors.

Financial Administration of Contracts, Including Payments

While the buyer wants the supplier to provide the contracted-for services on time and at a fair and reasonable price, the supplier wants to receive the contracted-for payment for work done and for funds expended in as timely a manner as possible. This discussion addresses procedures the buyer should undertake to assure suppliers are paid and the various cost-control measures buyers are expected to take, with explanations of how such measures differ by contract type.

Cost Control Measures for Different Types of Contracts

Different types of contracts create different financial relationships between the buyer and supplier. A firm-fixed-price contract provides the supplier with the strongest possible incentive to perform the contract in the most efficient manner. A supplier with this type of contract knows that every dollar under the estimated cost is a dollar added to profit. Under many types of contracts (cost-reimbursement contracts, among others), the supplier has little financial incentive to perform in the most efficient way since the buyer is reimbursing all reasonable, allowable, allocable costs. Moreover, the work description in cost-reimbursement contracts is usually broad because they are used when the buyer is not sure what he or she wants the supplier to do. In these contracts the supplier can often perform, and charge for, effort not contemplated by the buyer. The buyer and buyer's representative must be careful to administer these contracts in order to promote supplier economy and efficiency in funds management.

Firm-Fixed-Price Contracts
Under firm-fixed-price contracts and most other fixed-price contracts, there is no need for the buyer to get involved in supplier funds management. The supplier is obligated to perform the services for the firm-fixed-price, no matter whether he or she has overrun or underrun the estimated cost. A firm-fixed-price contract generally requires the supplier to tender for accep-

tance some discrete work deliverable in order to get paid. This does not necessarily mean the supplier cannot get paid until the work is completely done. A buyer can structure payments under a firm-fixed-price contract to permit payment on any of the following bases: (1) a lump-sum basis, with 100 percent of the payment made upon completion; (2) partial payments, with part of the total paid for delivery of part of the contracted work; (3) progress payments (progress payments can be based either on percentage or stage of completion or on costs incurred); or (4) advance payments (generally the least preferred method of payment). Each of these has its respective advantages and disadvantages.

Cost-Reimbursement Contracts

Under a cost-reimbursement contract, the buyer enters into a partnership with the supplier. As such, the buyer agrees to guide and direct supplier work efforts and funds management activities. Furthermore, the buyer may be permitted (particularly in the public sector) to disallow certain costs. The buyer in both the private and public sectors is entitled to ask the supplier for information needed to determine whether the expenses charged to the buyer are reasonable and allocable. Supplier costs must be reasonable and allocable before they can be reimbursed by the buyer.

Monitoring Supplier Costs

The buyer relies primarily on the buyer's representative to review supplier vouchers or invoices to identify waste. The buyer's representative should obtain whatever proof is necessary to satisfy the buying organization that the billing is legitimate. If the supplier fails to prove the legitimacy of the billings, the buyer should discuss the matter with the supplier. If the buyer believes the expense being charged is inappropriate, he or she should reduce the invoice or voucher by the amount of the questioned cost.

Exercising the Right to Disallow Costs

The buyer should have the contract right to disallow and not reimburse costs that are unreasonable in nature or amount. This right provides a powerful hammer over the supplier in their mutual effort to efficiently manage costs.

Administering a Typical Limitation of Cost/Funds
Provision

Every cost-reimbursement contract should contain either a "limitation of cost" provision or a "limitation of funds" provision. The limitation of funds provision is used for contracts that are incrementally funded. The limitation of cost provision is used for fully funded contracts.

Contents of the Typical Limitation of Cost/Funds
Provision
Limitation of cost/funds provisions generally stipulate that the supplier will
use its best efforts to perform the work within the negotiated cost ceiling
or estimate included in the contract. The supplier is generally not obligated
to perform any work in excess of the cost ceiling or estimate, nor is the
buyer obligated to pay for any such work. The buyer may decide to increase
the amount of funds applied to the contract in order to facilitate completion;
the buyer, however, has the sole contract right to increase the ceiling or
estimate.

Typical limitation of cost/funds provisions also require the supplier to
timely notify the buyer when the ceiling or estimate is about to be reached
and to provide a revised estimate of the total funding needed to complete the
contract work scope.

Reason for Using Limitation of Cost/Funds Provisions
Limitation of cost/funds (or similar) provisions are designed to avoid "funds
out" situations. Although they do this with some degree of exactitude, they
cannot provide a continuing picture of the status of contract funds. The buyer
and buyer's representative must track the supplier's cost of performance in
relation to the total estimated cost and keep the user or customer advised of
their findings.

Monitoring Costs
The buyer's representative should use the following techniques in administering a limitation of cost or funds provision:

1. The buyer's representative should evaluate all vouchers submitted by the
   supplier for obtaining reimbursement. These vouchers can provide a
   running total of costs incurred and billed.
2. Many contracts will require the supplier to submit periodic, interim
   financial reports. To be most useful, such reports should cover all aspects
   and phases of the budget for the entire project. Actual costs as stated in
   the report can be compared with planned costs to identify funding shortages so that timely management decisions regarding additional funding
   can be made.

The buyer and the buyer's representative should consider the following:

1. Once the total estimated cost or ceiling amount has been reached, the
   buyer cannot permit the supplier to continue work until additional funds
   have been provided. Obtaining funds may prove problematic.

2. Once the limitation of cost provision has relieved the supplier of the obligation to proceed, the buyer should not permit or condone continuation of supplier performance. Moreover, the buyer should not expect the supplier to maintain an indefinite state of readiness to resume performance.

3. The longer the fundless condition continues, the greater the risk that the supplier will disband his staff so that they will not longer be available to the contract. This would greatly increase the costs of resuming the work.

4. Gaps in performance force the user or customer to decide whether to seek funds to continue or terminate the contract, thus creating pressures that impede orderly and thorough exploration of alternatives. The resulting decisions may be hasty and ill-advised.

The better the funding information the buyer and buyer's representative can provide to the user/customer, the better able the user/customer will be to make sound decisions on the continued status of the contract. Early knowledge of the need for additional funds will enable the user department to avoid a gap in contract performance.

Once the supplier's performance costs have exceeded total estimated or ceiling costs and the supplier's obligation to proceed has been suspended, all buyer contract administration team members must avoid any action that would encourage the supplier to continue work and thus obligate the buyer to pay. Neither the buyer nor the buyer's representative have the authority to obligate funds in such a backhanded manner. The buyer or buyer's representative may be personally liable and responsible for this additional work.

Fairness and equity requires the buyer to promptly notify the supplier if the buying organization's decision is not to provide additional funds.

Administering Incrementally Funded Contracts
Ordinarily the need to obligate additional funds to a particular contract is unexpected. Some contracts, however, are expected from the beginning to require additional funding actions. Cost-reimbursement contracts, some fixed-price construction contracts, and some other categories of service contracts are incrementally funded. Incremental funding is particularly likely when the project is expected to be of more than a year's duration and the statement of work calls for discrete phases or increments.

An incrementally funded contract will use a limitation of funds provision rather than a limitation of cost provision. The user or customer will need to make the ultimate decision to apply additional funds to the contract. Before additional increments of work can be funded, the buyer and buyer's representative must apprise the customer of the supplier's performance on prior increments. At the customer's request, the buyer will issue a contract modification clearly stating the completion schedule for the new increment.

Payments

Authorizing Payment: Fixed-Price Versus Cost-Reimbursement
Payment is substantially simpler under fixed-price contracts than under most other types of contracts. To authorize payment under a fixed-price contract, the buyer or buyer's representative need only determine that the supplier has provided the required services. Under cost-reimbursement contracts (and some other flexibly price contracts) the buyer must pay allowable performance costs plus any fee required. The rules used to determine whether costs are allowable are discussed in the next section.

Cost-Reimbursement Contracts: Determining Allowable Costs
Only allowable costs are reimbursed under a cost-reimbursement contract. An allowable cost must be reasonable, allocable, in accordance with generally accepted cost-accounting standards and principles, and not specifically excluded by a provision in the contract.

Allowable Costs: Determining Reasonableness of Costs
A cost is reasonable if it does not exceed what a reasonably prudent businessperson would charge in a competitive environment. Particular care must be used in determining reasonableness when dealing with sole-source organizations or organizations otherwise not subject to effective competition. Asking the questions in Table 8-6 will help determine whether a cost is reasonable.

TABLE 8-6   Questions to ask in determining reasonableness of cost.

Cost type: Is the type of cost generally recognized as ordinary and necessary for the conduct of the supplier's business or the contract performance?

External restraints: What restraints or requirements are imposed by factors such as generally accepted sound business practices, arm's-length bargaining, and federal and state laws and regulations?

Prudent business practice: Would it be prudent business practice to allow the cost in light of the buyer's responsibilities to the owners of the business, the customers, the buyer's organization, and the general public?

Supplier's normal practices: Does the contract require sufficient deviation from the supplier's normal practices to justify an increase in the total contract cost?

The questions listed in Table 8-6 should be asked for both of the following areas:

1. The level of resources used (labor-hours, units of material, types of supplies, number of trips); and
2. The unit cost for each of those resources (wage rates, material unit costs, per diem rates, mileage rates, and so forth).

Allowable Costs: Determining Allocability of Costs

A cost is allocable if it is assignable or chargeable to one or more cost objectives on the basis of relative benefits received or other equitable relationships. Subject to the foregoing, a cost is allocable if it was incurred specifically for the contract, if it benefits both the contract and other work and can be distributed to them in reasonable proportion to the benefits received, or is necessary to the overall operation of the business (although a direct relationship to any particular cost objective cannot be shown). "Yes" answers to the questions in Table 8-7 will differentiate allocable from non-allocable costs.

Generally Accepted Accounting Principles and Practices

Generally accepted accounting principles and practices will ordinarily be the basis for evaluating cost elements and for determining allowable costs under cost-reimbursement contracts. The offeror's accounting principles and practices should be evaluated to ensure that accepted practice has been followed in applying values to such cost items as proposed salary schedules, material unit prices, depreciation costs, overhead allocation, and travel and lodging rates.

Many different principles and practices are acceptable. Although there are several different accounting methods (each one of which qualifies as a generally accepted accounting practice) for pricing inventory, for calculating depreciation cost, and for allocating overhead, each method results in a different cost calculation. The accounting method chosen should result in an equitable cost, one that is fair and reasonable to both the buyer and the supplier.

TABLE 8-7   Questions to determine allocability of cost.

Reason for the cost: Was the cost incurred specifically for the contract?
If the cost benefits both the contract and other work: Can it be distributed among the jobs it benefits in reasonable proportion to the benefits received?
If no direct relationship to a particular cost objective can be shown: Is the cost necessary to the overall operation of the supplier's business?

Allowability of Specific Items
Some buying organizations have policies and procedures containing a list of specific cost items that must be disallowed or that require special attention. Bad debts, contingencies, contributions and donations, entertainment, excess facility costs, fines and penalties, interest and other financial costs, and profit or loss on disposition of capital assets are often included in such lists. There are many other types of costs that a buying organization's policies and procedures may require a buyer to disallow.

Time-and-Materials and Labor-Hour Contracts
Authorizing payment under time-and-materials and labor-hour contracts involves considerations similar to those for cost-reimbursement contracts. Many of the differences stem from the fact that time-and-materials and labor-hour contracts typically include a negotiated hourly rate of compensation for each category of worker, as well as maxima and minima for the number of hours personnel in each category will be required to work. Normally the maximum number of hours represents a limit on the supplier's obligation. Since the buying organization has also agreed to a specific cost per hour, increasing the number of hours beyond the contractual maximum constitutes a change outside the scope of the contract and requires the supplier's assent. Under cost-reimbursement contracts the limitation of cost/funds provision gives the buyer the power to unilaterally increase the maximum number of hours by notifying the supplier of a cost estimate increase. This power is absent under time-and-materials and labor-hour contracts.

Although the buying organization is typically obligated to pay for all hours of work applied to the contract in good faith, the buyer's representative may still question an apparently excessive number of hours or an unnecessarily expensive labor category.

Using the supplier's management capabilities as one of the criteria for awarding the contract may help the buyer's representative persuade the supplier to avoid waste.

One excellent method of controlling costs on a time-and-materials or labor-hour contract is to order work on a fixed-price basis for each of the task or delivery orders provided to the service supplier. This method converts the contract to a series of fixed-price instruments and takes away the cost-reimbursement nature of the instrument.

Types of Payments

Regardless of the nature of the work or the contract type, a supplier will always need working capital: Money to meet payrolls, buy materials, pay subcontractors, and so forth. If sufficient cash or credit is not available, the supplier will go bankrupt before the work is completed. If the supplier's organization does not have enough cash internally, resources must be obtained elsewhere. Working capital is obtained through contract financing. Although private financing without direct buyer involvement is preferable, if such financing is insufficient or unavailable (and other conditions are met) the buyer may choose to make progress, partial, or advance payments. Providing such payments will increase the amount of contract administration required, thus increasing the total cost of the contract.

Progress Payments

Progress payments are incremental payments based on costs incurred by the supplier as work progresses under the contract. This form of financing does not include payments based on the percentage or stage of completion accomplished, payments for partial deliveries, or partial payments for contract-termination proposals. If the contract authorizes progress payments, the buying organization generally must pay the supplier based on the amount of monthly estimates approved by the buyer. The buyer should generally permit the buyer's representative to review and approve the request for progress payments. The supplier should be required to submit a contract cost breakdown for the buyer's approval on each progress payment. In making progress payments, the buyer may wish to retain as much as 10 percent of the estimated amount pending substantial completion of the work. As completion approaches, the buyer must release any portion of the retainage not needed to protect the buying organization.

The buyer is generally permitted to reduce or suspend progress payments under specified conditions, including noncompliance or unsatisfactory financial condition on the part of the supplier, excessive inventory, delinquent performance, or substantial loss.

Partial Payments

Progress payments are rare on service contracts (with the exception of construction contracts). Payment for services is usually made after performance of the required services. If multiple deliveries (partial performance) are possible, payment may be made after each delivery. Many organizations have a policy providing for partial payment following delivery valued in excess of either $1,000 or 50 percent of the contract price. Permitting buyers to allow payment "when the amount due so warrants" gives them discretion to provide for more frequent payment when necessary.

Advance Payments

Advance payments are monies made available to the supplier prior to work performance on the contract. Although advance payments may be made for any type of contract, they are very seldom used in service contracts.

Final Payment

Final payment under a contract is important. It completes the obligation of the buyer and also serves to cut off claim activities on the part of the supplier. Upon receiving final payment, the supplier gives up its right to engage in claims against the buying organization. Final payment also constitutes the final stage of the contract and permits the buyer to close out the contract.

The buyer should make a conscientious effort to settle any supplier claims before final payment. If the supplier submits a claim after final payment, the buyer must respond very carefully lest his or her response be interpreted as an admission that final payment was not intended to bar the claim.

The final payment voucher should always be accompanied by a certificate of contract completion, a final inspection report, a release of claims from the supplier, and a certification of payment.

Assignment of Claims

The buyer should not permit service suppliers to assign the monies due under a contract to any other person or organization unless the contract so permits. To aid service suppliers who wish to use their contract proceeds as collateral for bank financing, however, reasonable buyers should process assignments made to banks or other financial institutions. Such assignments must be made to a single financial institution for the full amount remaining on the contract at the time of assignment.

SUMMARY

Contract administration is the sum of actions taken by either the buyer's or the supplier's firm in assuring that each side fulfills its contractual agreement.

Routine Contract Administration

Routine contract administration is the body of administrative actions required for all service contracts. These actions include work control, assuring compliance with terms and conditions, financial control of the contract, and assuring quality of supplier systems/performance.

The Contract Administration Team

Contract administration is a team activity. The buyer is team captain, delegating tasks as needed. Team members most likely to be needed in service contract administration are the buyer's representative and the QAE.

A buyer's representative may act for the buyer in routine matters.

The QAE should monitor the quality and progress of the work, record his or her findings, and keep the buyer or buyer's representative informed.

Only the buyer should award contracts, modify contracts, delegate authority, obligate funds, cause the supplier to incur additional costs with the expectation of reimbursement, decide any matter that could invoke the disputes clause, or terminate the supplier's right to proceed.

The Contract Administration Plan

For each contract the buyer should prepare an administration plan covering the following issues for the entire life of the contract:

What must be done?
Who must do what?
Where, when, and how will contract activities take place?

Nonroutine Contract Administration

Work Ordering Under Some Contract Types

Work ordering and authorization are deferred until after award under the following types of contracts:

1. Indefinite-delivery type contracts,
2. Time-and-material/labor-hour contracts, and
3. Cost-reimbursement type contracts.
   Any postaward process is, by definition, a contract administration matter.

Contract Changes and Modifications

Administrative Change   A contract change not affecting the substantive rights or responsibilities of either party.

Cardinal Change   A change altering some essential element of the contract work.

Change Order   A written order, signed by the buyer, directing the supplier to implement a change authorized in the changes provision.

Contract Modification   A written alteration to an existing contract. There are unilateral and bilateral modifications.

Unilateral Modification   A contract change signed by only one party. Administrative changes and substantive changes authorized by the contract changes provision may be made unilaterally.

Bilateral Modification   A contract change signed by both parties.

Supplemental Agreement   A bilateral agreement used to make changes outside of the contract scope.

Changes Provision   This provision lists contract changes that the buyer may make unilaterally by means of a written order. Such changes will typically be within the scope of the contract.

Constructive Change   Constructive changes are oral, unilateral changes directed by a buying organization representative and implemented by the supplier.

Renewal Options

Renewal options are contract extension options provided for in the original contract and exercised unilaterally by the buyer. Quality of service and reasonableness of contract price should be the main factors in the decision to exercise extension options. The decision to exercise must be made before the contract expires.

Payments

Cost Control

Firm-fixed-price contracts provide strong incentive to perform the contract economically. Most labor-hour, time-and-materials, and cost-reimbursement contracts do not.

Firm-Fixed-Price Contracts   To authorize payment under firm-fixed-price contracts (and most other fixed-price contracts), the buyer need only be sure the work has been performed as described in the contract.

Cost-Reimbursement Contracts   Under a cost-reimbursement contract, the buyer must track and sometimes guide the supplier's cost-containment. The buyer may ask the supplier for any information needed to pursue this task. An allowable (reimbursable) cost must be:

1. Reasonable,
2. Allocable,
3. In accordance with generally accepted accounting principles, and
4. Not specifically excluded by contract provision.

Time-and-Materials and Labor-Hour Contracts   Time-and-material and labor-hour contracts involve considerations similar to those for cost-reimbursement contracts.

Types of Payments

When the supplier needs working capital and sufficient external financing is unavailable, the buyer may choose to make progress, partial, or advance payments. Such payments increase the cost of contract administration.

Progress Payments are incremental payments made on the basis either of costs incurred or percentage of completion.

Partial Payments are made after each delivery based on the percent of the total contract delivered.

Advance Payments are made prior to contract performance. They are extremely inappropriate for purchasing services.

Final Payment ends both the buying organization's obligation and any financing arrangement; it also cuts off supplier claims.

9

Claims, Terminations, and Disputes

Claims are defined as requests for additional compensation and/or extensions of contract performance time that do not originate from a recognized condition set forth in a contract provision. Contract provisions that sometimes lay the groundwork for a claim include changes, differing site conditions, and buyer-provided property. Table 9-1 contains a list of situations that tend to result in claims.

DIFFERING SITE CONDITIONS
AND SUSPENSIONS OF WORK

Claims resulting from differing site conditions and suspensions of work are governed by specific contract provisions. They are listed with claims not

TABLE 9-1   Situations often leading to supplier claims.

Differing site conditions.
Suspensions of work.
Defective specifications/statement of work.
Impossibility of performance.
Requiring a higher standard of performance than the contract.
Improper rejection of work performed.
Imposition of excessive test requirements.
Other constructive changes.
Late delivery of buyer-furnished material.
Interferences.
Failure to make work areas available.
Unreasonable delay in approval of shop drawings.
Other delays due to circumstances beyond the supplier's control.
Other actions or inactions of the buyer, which are alleged to be in nonconformance with the contract requirements.

governed by a contract provision because they require similar record-keeping and administrative procedures.

CLAIMS AVOIDANCE

The Basis of Claim Avoidance

Claim resolution is ordinarily complicated. The process is time-consuming and costly. It is in the best interests of both the buying organization and the supplier to take whatever steps are possible to avoid and/or minimize the necessity for claims.

Establishing a good relationship between the buying organization and the supplier sets the stage for claim avoidance. Good communications, clear channels of authority, clear directions, frequent supplier meetings, close coordination of all contract activities, accurate tracking of buyer-furnished material and equipment delivery, and prompt and proper interpretation and administration of the contract requirements will all improve buyer-supplier relations.

All buying-organization personnel should remain alert to the possibility of potential claims. The supplier should be encouraged to seek early resolution of any problems that might arise.

Specific Claim Avoidance Measures

Claim avoidance *per se* begins with a thorough review of the bid/proposal package to ensure contractibility. Reviews, however, do not end with contract award. Subsequent to award all personnel should continue to review the pertinent documents and additional data to resolve potential problems before they become significant.

Technical personnel should be reminded to make every effort to ensure prompt and accurate processing of supplier data submissions and requests for interpretation and/or clarification of specifications and drawings. When approvals of supplier data submissions are accompanied by comments, the comments should be carefully reviewed to determine if they include added requirements that are outside the scope of the contract. If requirements must be increased, the increases should be formally recognized and included in a written contract change.

Quality and project personnel should be instructed to refrain from encouraging the supplier to pursue options that may dilute or shift responsibility in the performance of the work. Any instructions, either written or oral, that buying-organization personnel find necessary to clarify or direct changes in the work scope should either be initiated or immediately ratified by written directions from the cognizant buyer.

Buyers must carefully monitor the transmittal of incoming and outgoing supplier data to ensure that delays in submissions, reviews and/or approvals are kept to a minimum. Buyer-furnished materials and/or equipment should also receive continual attention to ensure that contract commitment dates are met. If performance dates slip, the supplier should immediately be given written notification of the new performance dates and a written request for determination of any impact the expected delay may have.

Preparation for Defense of Claims

If events occur that could form the basis for a supplier's claim, legal counsel should be consulted so that the buying organization may prepare the best possible defense and mitigate any resultant liability costs.

All buyer personnel should maintain careful and complete records of their involvement in the work associated with the potential claim. Quality assurance evaluators and inspectors should be reminded to maintain daily logs complete with weather conditions; detailed descriptions of completed work; supplier's supervision, manpower, and equipment assigned to the work; and any other activities or events that may have an effect on work performance. Photographs depicting before and after conditions are especially valuable in preparing an effective defense.

All buyer personnel involved with the project should be cautioned that a potential claim is forthcoming. They should be told to refrain from making interpretations or offering suggestions that may affect the potential claim. They should avoid giving any indication either oral or written of acceptance of responsibility for the condition giving rise to the potential claim. Correspondence to and from the supplier should be carefully reviewed to determine any potential responsibility, eliminate any unnecessary requirements, and mitigate costs.

Resolution of Claims

The buyer must take the lead in providing a timely and businesslike treatment for every asserted claim. Common business courtesy and ethics require that claims be handled as expeditiously as possible. Failure to do so will result in justifiable criticism from the claimant.

As soon as a written claim has been received, the buyer should notify all interested parties within the buying organization, including legal counsel. Care should be taken to ensure that ensuing actions and discussions are kept within official channels. Buying organization employees should be encouraged to refrain from individual action that might enhance the supplier's position, and to avoid revealing information that might undermine their employer's ability to properly defend its position.

All claims should be promptly acknowledged in writing, stating that the claim has been received and is being taken under advisement. If the claim involves differing site conditions, contract requirements regarding prompt investigation and proper written direction on how to proceed should be implemented in a timely manner. Claims involving other contract provisions, such as suspension of work, will require differing actions on the part of the buyer. Any such actions deemed justified should be taken promptly.

All available information should be gathered and should initiate an investigation. Every effort should be made to develop complete and accurate findings that will support accurate evaluation of the validity of the supplier's claim. If the claim appears to have validity, the appropriate technical personnel should evaluate the circumstances to determine if there is continuing potential for further liability. If such potential exists, the buying organization should take whatever action is feasible to mitigate or eliminate any further exposure for increased costs (that is, fix the problem).

The buyer should maintain up-to-date chronological logs, minutes of all meetings, and all other data necessary for a complete and accurate history of the claim. Purchasing management should be kept informed of the current status of the claim.

The buyer should consider all relevant facts and prepare a detailed written recommendation on the appropriate course of action. This may require a request for additional clarification or supporting information from the supplier.

There are three ways for a buying organization to respond to a claim. The buying organization may treat the claim as follows:

1. Allow the claim;
2. Disallow the claim; or
3. Negotiate a division of responsibility for the claim and an equitable adjustment.

In the Event of Claim Acceptance

If the buying organization decides to allow all or part of the claim, a detailed cost estimate should be prepared and a negotiation position established. In developing a position for negotiation, expertise may be required from such functional areas of the buying organization as legal, accounting, quality assurance, engineering, and so forth. All relevant cost information should be used, including supplier's certified payrolls, previous audits, and data developed during previous negotiations.

For claims involving costs of delay, the buying organization should prepare time schedules that show concurrent delays and the relative effect the claimed delays had on the overall completion of the contract work. Computation of allowable increased costs should include any previous suspension or delay payments and payments made for overhead on changed and extra work. Since the purpose for any monetary payments in the claim cycle is to reimburse the supplier for increases in actual incurred costs, extreme care should be taken to avoid "windfall" or excess payment.

If the buying organization accepts the claim, prepares a negotiation position, and carries negotiations to a successful conclusion, the claim has been resolved by acceptance. If approval of the settlement is required, the claimant should be advised accordingly. After the settlement has been approved, the organization should issue a requisition covering the claim.

In providing the documentation for claims resolution, buyers should consider the *amount* of the claim, and respond accordingly (the higher the dollar amount, the greater the documentation). Many low-dollar claims can be quickly resolved, and in these cases, minimal documentation is required.

In the Event of Claim Rejection

If the buying organization decides to reject the claim, a written response should be prepared and submitted to the supplier with a detailed explanation. There are three courses of action available to the supplier upon receipt of a claim rejection.

1. Accept the rejection;
2. Disagree with the facts and submit additional data; or
3. Invoke the disputes procedure described in the contract.

If additional data is submitted, the review process should be reinitiated and another evaluation made of the claim's validity. The reopened investigation may result in another rejection letter, or it may result in a change in the buyer's position requiring further negotiation.

Disputes are time-consuming and costly to both sides. A reasonable effort should be made to dispose of claims through the negotiation process. On the other hand, if the buying organization considers its position sound, it should not hesitate to maintain that position in the face of a possible dispute.

All cognizant buyer personnel should keep in mind that claims generally require management approval prior to issuance of any procurement document. Additionally, the buyer's counsel must generally review and/or approve all claim resolutions.

TERMINATIONS

Definitions

Complete Termination   The complete cessation of all contracted work that had not been completed and accepted on or before the effective date of termination.

Partial Termination   The termination of a portion, but not all, of the contracted work that had not been completed and accepted on the effective date of termination.

Termination Inventory   Any property purchased, supplied, manufactured, furnished, or otherwise acquired for the performance of a contract subsequently terminated and properly allocable to the terminated portion of the contract. It includes buyer-furnished property.

A Temporary Stoppage of Work   A hiatus in the work due to a stop work order from the buyer—*not a termination.*

Reductions in the scope of work resulting from an engineering change and settled under a bilateral agreement are also not terminations.

Termination Procedures

Mutual Cancellation

Before issuing a formal notice of termination, the buyer shall, whenever possible, undertake to negotiate a settlement with the supplier. In many cases such negotiations will result in a relatively simple walk-away agreement. Once a formal notice of termination is issued, the more complicated formal termination process may have to be followed to its conclusion.

Termination for Convenience

Contracts/purchase orders should be terminated for the convenience of the buying organization when it is determined that such action is in its best interests.

Written Notice of Termination

If the buying organization decides to issue a formal notice of termination, the buyer must prepare a written notice specifying the items listed in Table 9-2.

The buyer must follow through on the termination notice and ensure that all work is stopped as stated in the notice in order to avoid the need to disallow costs incurred thereafter. It may not be possible to stop all costs on the day of the notice despite all reasonable efforts to do so. Certain costs for storing and protecting inventory items may be required after termination. Prompt and clear communications with the supplier should smooth transition to termination.

TABLE 9-2   Items needed in written notice of termination for convenience.

Statement: The contract is terminated for the convenience of the buying organization. List the contract provision that authorizes such action.
Effective date of the termination.
Extent of termination.
Special instructions.
Steps the supplier may take to minimize the impact on personnel if the termination, together with all other outstanding terminations, will result in a significant reduction in the supplier's work force.

Handling Termination Inventory

The buying organization should verify the amount of termination inventory in the hands of the supplier and its subcontractors immediately after issuing notice of termination. The inventory should be screened to determine how much of it is serviceable and usable. Then, with the approval of the buyer's property manager, the supplier and buying organizations should agree to undertake the steps outlined in Table 9-3 in the indicated order of priority.

Posttermination Discussions

At the earliest reasonable date following termination, the buyer should initiate a meeting with the supplier. In preparation for the meeting, the buyer should become thoroughly familiar with the termination for convenience provision of the contract and should have a working knowledge of the buying organization's policy for such terminations. A checklist of topics for discussion at the meeting is outlined in Table 9-4.

Subcontractor Claims Against the Supplier

It is the supplier's responsibility to settle subcontractor claims, and these subcontractors should not make direct claims against the buyer.

All termination claims should be submitted on either an inventory or total cost basis. The total amount payable to the supplier on a fixed-price termi-

TABLE 9-3   Recommended measures for handling termination inventory.

The buying organization will acquire the inventory it chooses.
The supplier will purchase or retain at cost the items it will accept.
The supplier will return as many of the remaining items as possible to its suppliers for full credit less the supplier's normal restocking charge, or 25 percent, whichever is less.
The supplier will sell or make other disposition of items as agreed to.
Proceeds from property sales, retentions, or restocking will be credited to the contract. Property sales will generally require competitive bids from potential buyers.

TABLE 9-4   Topics to resolve following termination for convenience.

Supplier termination claims: General principles relating to settlement of any termination claim.

Supplier obligations: Obligations of the supplier under the termination provision of the contract.

Extent of termination.

The point at which the work is stopped.

Status of plans, drawings, and other data that were to be delivered under the contract.

Status of any work that was not terminated.

Subcontractors: Names of subcontractors and dates when termination notices were sent to them.

Subcontractor claims: Supplier's method of reviewing and settling subcontractor claims.

Termination inventory: General principles and procedures to be followed to protect, preserve, and dispose of inventory in the hands of the supplier and its subcontractors.

Settlement proposals and supporting data: The format in which settlement proposals, inventory schedules, and accounting data will be submitted.

Settlement proposals and supporting data: Tentative time schedules for submitting proposals, inventory schedules, and other data.

nation settlement should not exceed the total contract price, exclusive of settlement costs.

Termination for Default or Cause

Every contract must cover the possibility of termination for default or cause. Justifications for default/cause termination generally include:

(1) "If the Supplier fails to make delivery of the supplies or to perform the services within the time specified herein or any extension thereof"; or

(2) "If the Supplier fails to perform any of the other provisions of the contract, or so fails to make progress as to endanger performance of the contract in accordance with its term...."

Written Notice of Termination for Default or Cause

The buyer is generally required to give the supplier ten days notice in writing (cure notice) before terminating for default under the second condition stated above.

Before issuing the notice of termination, the buyer must be thoroughly familiar with the termination for default provision stated in the contract being terminated. Such provisions generally make the supplier liable for excess costs, the transfer of title to completed work, and causes that excuse the supplier from liability for excess costs.

Alternative Actions

Even when the supplier has clearly defaulted, complete termination for default may not be in the best interests of the buying organization. Before terminating a contract for default, the buyer should consider both the issues outlined in Table 9-5 and the alternatives listed in Table 9-6. The buyer should choose the course of action that most benefits the buying organization.

DISPUTES

Every contract or purchase order should contain a provision delineating procedures for resolving issues in dispute. In most cases the best course of action is to negotiate with the supplier. A mechanism must be in place, however, to resolve issues that cannot be resolved through negotiation.

Although the courts are available for dispute resolution, many organizations have found mediation or arbitration less costly and more expedient mechanisms. Arbitration normally calls for one or more (the norm is three) independent, impartial conflict resolution experts. Many individuals selected for such assignments are either retired administrative or legal judges or are individuals who have otherwise developed an ability to find common ground between adverse interests. There are a number of arbitration organizations that offer their services to resolve disputes according to their rules. The most well known arbitration organization is the American Arbitration Associa-

---

TABLE 9-5   Issues to consider before terminating a contract for default or cause.

Causes of nonperformance: The specific reasons for the supplier's failures and excuse for non-performance.

Availability of services: Whether needed services are available from other sources.

Relative time frames: The urgency of the need and the lead time required to obtain the materials or services from another source.

Termination effects: The effect of the termination on the supplier and how essential the supplier is to the buyer's purchasing program.

TABLE 9-6   Alternatives to complete termination for default or cause.

Revise the delivery schedule: Permit the supplier or the supplier's surety or guarantor to continue performance under a revised delivery schedule.

Third-party arrangements: Permit the supplier to continue performance by means of a business arrangement with some other acceptable third party, provided the buyer's rights are adequately preserved.

Mutual cancellation: Execute a bilateral no-cost termination if the requirement is no longer needed and the supplier is not liable for damages.

---

tion. Although arbitration services are not free, they provide a more timely and often less expensive alternative to the courts.

It is important to remember that there must be a legal forum available to interpret whether arbitration is applicable as well as to enforce the judgments of the arbitration body. This fact should encourage buyers to have their legal counsel include appropriate provisions dealing with "choice of legal forum" and "choice of law" in service contracts.

SUMMARY

Supplier Claims

Claims are requests for added compensation and/or performance time extensions not covered by any contract provision. Such requests caused by differing site conditions and suspensions of work are governed by contract provisions, but are still considered claims because they require similar administrative procedures. Settling claims is usually a time-consuming and expensive process.

Claims Avoidance

The basis of claim avoidance is a good supplier-buying organization relationship. Buying-organization personnel should cooperate with the supplier and avoid giving instructions that could be outside the scope of the contract. Claim avoidance measures should include reviewing the bid/proposal package to ensure contractibility. Other pertinent documents and data should be reviewed continually to identify and resolve problems early.

Preparation for Defense of Claims

If a claim is in the offing, legal counsel should be consulted immediately and buyer personnel involved with the project should be warned. They should maintain complete records of their involvement with the work and supplier, and avoid giving any indication of acceptance of responsibility. Correspondence to and from the supplier should be carefully reviewed.

Resolution of Claims

Claims should be treated in a businesslike fashion. All appropriate actions should be implemented promptly. As soon as a written claim is received the buyer should notify all interested parties within the buying organization, including legal counsel, and acknowledge the claim in writing. Buying organization employees should avoid individual actions or statements, keeping ensuing actions and discussions within official channels.

The buyer should maintain an up-to-date, complete, and accurate history of the claim and keep purchasing management informed. An investigation should be initiated to discover whether the supplier's claim has merit. The buyer should write a detailed recommendation on whether the claim should be allowed, disallowed, or negotiated and equitably adjusted.

If the Claim Is Accepted
A detailed cost estimate should be prepared, a negotiation position established, and an equitable adjustment negotiated.

If the Claim Is Rejected
A written response should be prepared and submitted to the supplier explaining the reasons for rejection. The supplier can respond as follows: accept the rejection, disagree with the facts and submit additional data, or invoke the disputes provision of the contract. If additional data is submitted, the review process should be reinitiated. As disputes are time-consuming and costly to both sides, reasonable effort should be made to dispose of claims through negotiation.

Termination Procedures
Mutual Cancellation
In most cases, buyers should attempt to negotiate informal walk-away agreements with the supplier before issuing a formal notice of termination. Once formal notice of termination is issued, the more complicated formal termination process may have to be followed to conclusion.

Termination for Convenience
A termination for convenience is undertaken in the buying organization's best interests rather than for supplier default. If the buying organization issues a formal notice of termination, the buyer must prepare written notice. The buyer must ensure that all work is stopped as stated in the notice in order to avoid having to disallow costs incurred thereafter.

The buying organization should determine the amount of termination inventory held by the supplier and its subcontractors immediately after issuing a notice of termination to facilitate equitable disposition of inventory.

The buyer should initiate termination negotiations with the supplier as soon as possible after issuing the termination notice. The total amount paid to the supplier in a fixed-price termination settlement should not exceed the total contract price, exclusive of settlement costs. The supplier must settle subcontractor claims.

Termination for Default or Cause

Termination for default or cause should be covered in the contract, with justifications for such terminations listed therein. Normal justifications include failure of the supplier to perform or failure to progress rapidly enough to allow completion on time.

Before terminating a contract for default, the buyer should consider the reasons for the supplier's nonperformance and the difficulties that would result from trying to procure the service elsewhere. Other actions that may serve the interests of the buying organization better than termination for default include continued performance under a revised timetable or a negotiated, "no-fault" termination.

Disputes

Although the best way to resolve disputes is generally to negotiate with the supplier, every contract or purchase order needs a mechanism to resolve issues that cannot be resolved through negotiation.

Many organizations have found arbitration or mediation to be less costly and more expedient mechanisms than the courts. Arbitration normally calls for one or more (the norm is three) independent, impartial conflict resolution experts. Choice of legal forum and choice of law should be specified in service contracts even if mediation or arbitration is the dispute method for which the contract provides.

10

Evaluating Supplier Performance and Closing Out Contracts

SERVICE SUPPLIER PERFORMANCE EVALUATIONS

Supplier performance evaluations are valuable documents and should be prepared in a careful, conscientious manner. It is extremely important that they be based on factual rather than subjective data. Evaluation reports are often used to determine whether to solicit incumbent suppliers for follow-up work and are used in conjunction with other information to select suppliers for other, subsequent work.

The evaluation forms are normally completed at the time of final payment and release. If the buyer intends to render either an unsatisfactory or outstanding evaluation, he or she should send a preliminary copy of the report to the supplier by mail. The supplier should be permitted to comment on the contents of the report and any rebuttal should be included in or attached to the report.

CLOSEOUTS OF SERVICE CONTRACTS

The buyer is responsible for initiating any correspondence with the supplier necessary to secure the documents and information required to close out the contract. This action is taken immediately upon completion of service delivery and subsequent acceptance by the buyer. The buyer is responsible for all follow-up actions required to ensure that the supplier receives all the necessary correspondence.

A chronological sequence for closeout is outlined in Table 10-1.

TABLE 10-1   Closeout sequence.

Purchase order or contract review: Review the purchase order or contract in its entirety to ensure that the supplier has complied with all requirements.

Closeout information checklist: Prepare and file information required for items listed on a service supplier closeout checklist. (A typical service contract closeout checklist is found at Appendix J.)

Documentation due from the supplier: Determine applicable documentation required of the supplier and obtain this documentation for the file.

SUMMARY

Performance Evaluations

Supplier evaluations, normally completed at the time of final payment and release, are used to determine whether to solicit the supplier for later business. They should be based on objective rather than subjective data. The supplier should receive a preliminary copy of either outstanding or unfavorable evaluations and should be allowed to append comments to the final report.

Service Contract Closeout

The buyer is responsible for ensuring that all documents required for closeout, from either the supplier or the buyers own organization, reach their required destinations.

Chronological Sequence

1. Ensure that the supplier has complied with all requirements of the contract or purchase order.
2. Prepare and file all documents the buying organization must provide for closeout.
3. Determine and obtain documentation required of the supplier.

CONCLUSION

Buyers of supplies and buyers of services share the same basic objectives of quality, timely delivery or performance, and fair and reasonable prices. Situationally required differences in approach and methodology, however, make their purchasing tasks separate and distinct. The buyer of supplies is advised to heed these differences before venturing into the business of buying services. Buyers should not be intimidated by that prospect. Rather, they should take solace in the fact that well-rounded buyers have generally started from a supply orientation, later expanding into service purchasing and other specialty buying. This book was designed to provide you with the tools you need to make that transition.

References

Aljian, George W. and Farrell, Paul V. *Aljian's Purchasing Handbook*. 4th ed. New York: McGraw-Hill, 1982.

Award, Administration, and Surveillance of Service Type Contracts. Virginia Beach, Va. Director, Naval Audit Service Southeast Region, 1982.

Award and Administration of Service Contracts, U.S. Army Europe and Seventh Army. Alexandria, VA: The Auditor General, U.S. Army Audit Agency, 1988.

Brooks, Daniel T. *Computer Law: Purchasing, Leasing, and Licensing Hardware, Software, and Services*. New York, N.Y.: Purchasing Law Institute, 1980.

Brusman, Calvin. *Best Value Source Selection—Made Easy*. 1991 NAPM International Purchasing Conference Proceedings. Tempe, Az.: National Association of Purchasing Management, 1991.

Contract Administration for Technical Personnel and Project Managers, Norfolk, Va.: Kalman and Company, Inc., 1988.

Controls Over DOD's Management Support Service Contracts Need Strengthening. Washington, D.C.: U.S. General Accounting Office, 1981.

DCAA Contract Audit Manual. Washington, D.C.: Government Printing Office, 1991.

Demone, Harold W. and Margaret Gibelman. *Services for Sale*. New Brunswick: Rutgers University Press, 1989.

Davies, G.J. and Gray, R. *Purchasing International Freight Services*. Brookfield, Vt.: Gower, 1985.

Dobler, Donald W., Lamar Lee, Jr., and David N. Burt. *Purchasing and Materials Management*, 5th Edition. New York: McGraw-Hill Book Company, 1990.

Dobler, Donald W., Lamar Lee, Jr., and David N. Burt. *Purchasing and Materials Management*, 4th Edition. New York: McGraw-Hill Book Company, 1984.

Federal Acquisition Regulation (FAR). Washington, D.C.: Government Printing Office, 1992.

Federal Register. Washington, D.C.: Government Printing Office, 1991.

Gazarek, George and Rose. *The Essence of Government Contract Management* (A six-cassette audiocassette program). Private Publication. 1989.

Graw, LeRoy H. *Service Contracting? Let's Not Get Personal Here!* 1991 NAPM International Purchasing Conference Proceedings. Tempe, Az.: National Association of Purchasing Management, 1991.

Guide to Government Contracting. Chicago, Il.: Commerce Clearing House, 1991.

Heberling, Michael. *Negotiating Changes Before They Occur.* 1990 NAPM International Purchasing Conference Proceedings. Tempe, Az.: National Association of Purchasing Management, 1990.

Heinritz, Stuart F., Paul V. Farrell and Larry Guinipero. *Purchasing: Principles and Applications,* 8th Edition. Englewood Cliffs, NJ: Prentice-Hall, 1991.

Hirsch, William J. *The Contracts Management Deskbook,* Revised Edition. American Management Association.

How to Improve Installation Support Services. Bethesda, Md.: Logistics Management Institute, 1989.

Kendrick, John L. "The Service Industries' Tools." *Quality* (October 1986): 12–17.

Kettner, Peter M. *Purchase of Service Contracting.* Newbury, Ca.: Sage Publications, 1987.

Langmaid, Michelle C. *The Great Divorce in Contracting: Termination for Convenience.* 1990 NAPM International Purchasing Conference Proceedings. Tempe, Az.: National Association of Purchasing Management, 1990.

Leavitt, Preston J. *Buying Service: Learning to Cope With Lions & Tigers & Bears.* 1991 NAPM International Purchasing Conference Proceedings. Tempe, Az.: National Association of Purchasing Management, 1991.

Leenders, Michiel R., Harold E. Fearon and Wilbur B. England. *Purchasing and Materials Management,* 9th Edition. Homewood, Il.: Irwin, 1989.

Office of Federal Procurement Policy (OFPP) Proposed Policy Letter 92, Subject: *Management Oversight of Service Contracting,* dated December 20, 1991. Washington, D.C.: Government Printing Office, 1991.

Reddington, Albert S. *Buying Consultant Services.* 1990 NAPM International Purchasing Conference Proceedings. Tempe, Az.: National Association of Purchasing Management, 1990.

Review of DOD Contracts Under OMB Circular A-76. Washington, D.C.: U.S. General Accounting Office, 1981.

Scheuing, Eberhard. *Purchasing Management.* Englewood Cliffs, N.J.: Prentice-Hall, 1989.

Sherman, Stanley N. *Contract Management: Post Award.* Germantown, Md.: Wordcrafters Publications, 1987.

Smarter Contracting for Installation Support Services. Bethesda, Md.: Logistics Management Institute, 1986.

Standard Industrial Classification Manual. Washington, D.C.: Government Printing Office, 1987.

The Handbook of Effective Contract Management. Richmond, Va.: Caldwell Consulting Associates, 1985.

United States Army Logistics Management Center, Fort Lee, Va. *Type of Contracts Summary, ALM 33-3350-H.*, undated.

United States Postal Service, Washington, D.C. *Contract Administration Reference Guide.* Prepared by Educational Services Institute under Contract No. 104220-85-H-001, © Educational Services Institute, updated.

Whitman, Earl K. *Contracting for Consultant Services.* 1990 NAPM International Purchasing Conference Proceedings. Tempe, Az.: National Association of Purchasing Management, 1990.

Zemansky, Stanley D. *Contracting Professional Services.* 1991 NAPM International Purchasing Conference Proceedings. Tempe, Az.: National Association of Purchasing Management, 1991.

Appendix A

The Service Contract Act

I. The Service Contract Act applies in accordance with the processes of 29 CFR PART 4 to public contracts "the principal purpose of which is to furnish services through the use of service employees." The Act applies to both white collar and blue collar workers, other than bona fide executive, administrative and professional workers, and includes clerical, technical, and lower level computer data input personnel. The Act expressly excludes the following types of subcontracts:

A. Construction, alteration and repair, including painting and decorating, of public buildings or public works.

B. Work subject to Walsh-Healey Public Contracts Act (that is, manufacturing).

C. Transportation where published tariff rates are in effect.

D. Communications subject to the Communications Act of 1934.

E. Any subcontract for public utility services.

F. Employment contracts by federal agencies.

G. Postal contract services for the Postal Service.

H. Services to be performed entirely outside the United States.

I. Maintenance, calibration and/or repair of:

(1) ADPE and office information/word processing systems;

(2) Scientific equipment and medical apparatus or equipment where the application of microelectronic circuitry or similar technology is an essential element; and

(3) Office/business machines where the work is performed by the manufacturer or supplier of the equipment.

II. The following are examples (a nonexclusive list) of contracts that are subject to the Act:

A. Custodial, janitorial, housekeeping, and guard services.

B. Laundry, dry cleaning, linen supply, and clothing repair services.

C. Some support services, including grounds maintenance and landscaping.

D. Certain specialized services requiring specific skills, such as drafting, stenographic services, and mortuary services.

E. Packing, crating, and storage.

F. Food service and lodging.

G. Snow, trash, and garbage removal.

H. Mail hauling, motor pool operation, parking, taxicab, and ambulance services.

I. Aerial spraying and aerial reconnaissance for fire detection.

J. Geotechnical data gathering.

K. Archaeological clearances and surveying work (including topological and aerial surveying).

III. *Responsibilities*:

A. Buyers are responsible for:

(1) Including the standard FAR Service Contract Act provision in all contracts and purchase orders over $2,500 that are subject to the Act;

(2) Including the following provision in contracts and orders under $2,500 that are subject to the Act:

"SERVICE CONTRACT ACT OF 1965 - (FOR ORDERS FOR NON-PROFESSIONAL SERVICES $2,500 OR LESS)

"Except to the extent that an exemption, variation, or tolerance would apply if this Contract were in excess of $2,500, the Contractor and any subcontractor shall pay all of its employees engaged in performing work on the contract not less than the minimum wage specified under Section 6(a)(1) of the Fair Labor Standards Act of 1938, as amended. (29 U.S.C. 201–206) Regulations and interpretations of the Service Contract Act of 1965, as amended, are contained in 29 CFR Part 4."

(3) Including the following provision in contracts and orders that utilize fewer than five service employees in the performance of the contract work:

"This involves work covered under the 'Service Contract Act of 1965,' as amended; *provided however*, if you utilize fewer than five service employees in the performance of the contract work, the wage determination for the Service Contract Act cited above, does *not* apply and the Fair Labor Standards Act minimum wage requirements are applicable to this Contract."

(4) Submitting Standard Forms 98 and 98a "Notice of Intention to Make a Service Contract and Response Notice" (properly executed) to DOL Headquarters in Washington, D.C., in order to obtain the appropriate wage rates to include in the solicitation and resulting contract.

IV. *Procedures*

A. Buyers shall submit the completed Standard Form 98 and 98a to DOL prior to issuing an RFP/RFQ that meets the criteria above. The SF 98 form must show the classes of employees and the number of each class (see Service Contract Act Directory of Occupations for classification and numeric code). All SF 98's and SF 98A's should be submitted at least sixty (60) days prior to issuing an RFP/RFQ to assure timely completion of all reviewing and determination authority.

B. If circumstances prevent timely filing of the Notice of Intention, it should be submitted as soon as possible with an explanation of the circumstances which delayed submission.

C. If the services are substantially the same as those now being performed by an incumbent contractor whose contract the proposed contract will succeed, the buyer must include a copy of any collective bargaining agreement and related documents which specify wage rates and fringe benefits along with the Form 98 and 98A.

D. Extending an existing contract, under an option clause or otherwise, creates a new contract for purposes of the Act and requires the new submittal of Forms 98 and 98A.

E. The Labor Department will issue wage determinations in response to the Form 98 and 98A, and this determination shall be attached to the RFP/RFQ distributed to offerors. The determination should also be attached to the resulting contract when awarded.

F. The buyer shall instruct the Contractor to post a Department of Labor poster WH-1313, Notice to Employees Working on Government Contracts, which is required by regulation, and to either post in a prominent place at the work site a copy of the wage determination listing all minimum wages and fringe benefit as specified in the contract, or to deliver a copy of the wage determination to each service employee on the date that employee commences work on the service contract.

G. Buyers shall, upon request of the Department of Labor, withhold from contract payments the amounts needed to pay underpaid employees. Any contractor who fails to comply with the requirements of the Act is subject to termination of the contract for default. In addition, any such contractor may become ineligible for award of Government contracts and subcontracts.

Appendix B

Laws Governing Public Sector Construction Contracting

1. The Davis-Bacon Act applies to "contracts "of $2,000 or greater, to which the United States or the District of Columbia is a party for construction, alteration, or repair (including painting and decorating) of public buildings or public works...." The Act applies to laborers or mechanics employed directly upon the site of the work and states that the classification of labor identified shall receive no less than the prevailing wage rate including fringe benefits as determined by the Secretary of Labor.
2. The Copeland Act "makes it unlawful to induce, by force, intimidation, threat of procuring dismissal from employment, or otherwise, any person employed in the construction or repair of public buildings or public works, financed in whole or in part by the United States, to give up any part of the compensation to which that person is entitled under a contract of employment."
3. The Contract Work Hours and Safety Standard Act—Overtime Compensation applies when the contract may require or involve the employment of labor and mechanics for construction contracts greater than $2,000 or contracts other than construction greater than $2,500. The Act provides for compensation to laborers and mechanics for overtime, work of more than 40 hours in any work week, at a rate of $1\frac{1}{2}$ times the basic rate of pay for all additional hours.
4. The Copeland Act and the Contract Work Hours and Safety Standard Act—Overtime Compensation are known as the "Related Acts" and apply to all construction contracts.
5. The following type work is excluded from coverage by the Davis-Bacon and Related Acts:
   a. Work defined as "an incidental amount of work"—"work directly related to the installation, movement, or rearrangement of equipment

or machinery, relatively small in amount, and which does not include changes in a facility affecting its architectural or structural strength, stability, safety, size, or function as a public work."

b. Contracts for furnishing supplies and equipment, including installation, where the installation requires only an incidental amount of work that would otherwise be considered construction, alteration, and/or repair.

c. Contracts for servicing or maintenance work in an existing facility (plant) including installation or movement of machinery or other equipment, and facility (plant) rearrangement, which involves only an incidental amount of work that would otherwise be considered construction, alteration and/or repair.

d. Contracts for operational or maintenance activities (that is, production, research & development, or community services, are distinguished from contracts for construction).

e. Contracts for demolition except when performed on a phase of a covered construction project or when subsequent construction activity at the site being cleared is contemplated.

f. Contracts with a state or a subdivision thereof.

g. Contracts with a railroad for construction services to the extent that the services are performed by employees covered by the Railway Labor Act.

h. Recurring maintenance work to roads and parking lots such as patching surfaces, filling chuck-holes, patching shoulders, and resurfacing railroad damages.

i. Where determination of noncoverage is based on material risk to continuity of operations, to life or property, or to operating requirements.

6. Examples of work covered by the Davis-Bacon and Related Acts

a. Work performed by laborers and mechanics employed by a construction contractor or subcontractor at the site of the work under a contract for the construction, alteration and/or repair, including painting and decorating, which is otherwise subject to the Davis-Bacon and Related Acts whether or not such work would be covered if it were a separate contract.

b. Construction of roads, including grading, and their repair where such repair includes work in roadways before resurfacing, building shoulders, forming ditches, culverts and bridges, and on the actual resurfacing of roads.

c. All work for installation, rearrangement or adjustment of equipment during construction of a new facility (plant) in an integral part of the construction project that permits the facility to be used for the purpose intended whether or not in the scope of the contract.

7. The buyer is responsible for:
   a. Including clauses at FAR 22.407 in all contracts and purchase orders over $2,000 that are subject to the Davis-Bacon Act;
   b. Including the following clause in contracts and orders under $2,000 that are subject to the Davis-Bacon and Related Acts.

      "Davis-Bacon and Related Acts - (For Orders of Construction of $2,000 or Less)."

      "Except to the extent that an exemption, variation, or tolerance would apply if this Contract were in excess of $2,500, the Contractor and any subcontractor shall pay all of its' employees engaged in performing work on the contract not less than the minimum wage specified under Section 6(a)(1) of Fair Labor Standards Act of 1938, as amended (29 U.S.C. 201–206). Regulations and interpretations of the Davis-Bacon and Related Acts, as amended, are contained in 29 CFR Parts 1,3, and 5."
   c. Assuring that the appropriate wage determination is contained in each solicitation for construction. The appropriate wage determination shall be a material part of the contract or purchase order.
   d. Requiring the contractor to provide weekly SF 347's and SF 348's or other acceptable reports containing the same information and certification required at 29 CFR Part 3 for all laborers and mechanics employed under the resulting contract or purchase order to include all subcontracts.
   e. Assuring that all labor covered by Davis-Bacon and Related Acts is properly classified, that hours worked are properly reflected, that all wages are paid, that all overtime is computed properly and paid, and that withholding practices are consistently used.
   f. Submitting Standard Form 308 "Request for Determination and Response to Request" properly executed, to DOL for coordination of notice requirements.
8. *Procedures*
   a. A buyer or designated representative must, 60 days prior to issuance of an IFB or RFP that is for construction, alternation, or repair (including painting or decorating), submit the SF-308 to DOL.
   b. A buyer or designated representative must assure that each SF-308 submitted contains a sufficiently detailed description of the work to indicate the type of construction involved, identify the type of project and the county and state where the work is to be performed. Further, due to the unique requirements of the initial construction and subsequent systems installation, additional descriptions or separate attachments necessary for clarification and/or verification of the determination authority shall be provided.

c. If circumstances prevent a timely filing of the SF-308, they should be submitted with an explanation of the circumstances that delayed submission.

d. Submission of the SF-308 shall be made irrespective of any general wage rate determinations applicable to the project.

e. In the case of contracts entered into pursuant to competitive bidding procedures, modification of wage determinations received by the buyer less than ten days before the opening of bids shall be effective unless there is a finding by the head of the Purchasing Office or his or her designated representative that there is not reasonable time still available before bid opening to notify bidders of the modification of the wage determination and a report of the finding inserted into the contract file. No such report shall be required if the modification funding is received after bid opening.

f. Modifications or superseding wage determinations to an applicable general wage determination published after contract award (or after the beginning of construction where there is no contract award) shall not be effective except:

   If the contract has not been awarded within ninety (90) days after bid opening; or

   If construction has not begun within ninety (90) days after initial endorsement or the signing of the agreement, any modification published in the Federal Register prior to the award of the contract or the beginning of construction, as appropriate, shall be effective with respect to the contract unless the head of the Purchasing Office or his or her designated representative requests and obtains an extension of the ninety (90) day period.

g. Should a wage determination not be available within the prescribed period prior to final award or if the wage determination is found to be incorrect or if the Davis-Bacon Act clearly does not apply to the contract, the buyer shall, at the direction of the head of the Purchasing Office or his or designated representative, either:

   Terminate and resolicit the contract with the valid determination; or

   Incorporate the valid wage determination retroactive to the beginning of construction through supplemental agreement; or

   Through a change order, incorporate the valid wage determination, provided that the contractor is compensated for any increase in wages resulting from such a change order; or

   Incorporate the valid wage determination and adjustment in the contract price, where appropriate, in accordance with applicable procurement and contracting standard practices of the buyer's organization.

Appendix C

Work Words

Analyze—solve by analysis.

Annotate—provide with comments.

Ascertain—find out with certainty.

Attend—be present at.

Audit—officially examine.

Build—make by putting together.

Calculate—find out by computation.

Consider—think about; decide.

Construct—put together; build.

Control—direct; regulate.

Contribute—give along with others.

Compare—evaluate likeness or difference.

Create—cause to be; make.

Determine—resolve; settle; decide.

Differentiate—make a distinction between.

Develop—bring into being; activate.

Define—make clear; set the limits.

Design—make an original plan.

Evolve—develop gradually; work out.

Examine—look at closely; test quality of.

Explore—examine for discovery.

Extract—take out; deduce; select.

Erect—put together; set upright.

Establish—set up; settle; prove beyond dispute.

Estimate—form an opinion of the quantity or amount.

Evaluate—find or fix the value of.

Fabricate—build; manufacture; invent.

Form—give shape to; establish.

Formulate—put together and express.

Generate—produce; cause to be.

Install—put into position.

Inspect—examine carefully or officially.

Institute—set up; establish; begin.

Interpret—explain the meaning of.

Inquire—ask; make a search of.

Integrate—add parts to make a whole.

Investigate—search into; examine closely.

Judge—decide; form an estimate of.

Make—cause to be.

Manufacture—fabricate from raw materials or components.

Notice—comment upon; review.

Observe—inspect; watch.

Originate—initiate; give rise to.

Organize—integrate; arrange in a coherent unit.

Perform—do; carry out; accomplish.

Plan—devise a scheme for doing, making, arranging activities to achieve objectives.

Probe—investigate thoroughly.

Produce—give birth or rise to.

Pursue—seek, obtain or accomplish.

Reason—think; use arguments to influence another's actions.

Resolve—reduce by analysis; clear up.

Record—set down in writing or electronic communications media.

Recommend—advise; attract favor of.

Review—inspect; examine; evaluate.

Study—careful examination or analysis.

Seek—try to discover; attempt.

Search—examine to find something.

Scan—look through hastily; examine intently.

Solve—find an answer.

Trace—copy; find by following a trail.

Track—observe or plot the path of.

Appendix D

Ambiguous Terms

1. All reasonable requests of the buyer shall be complied with.
2. As determined by the buyer.
3. As directed by the buyer.
4. Carefully performed.
5. Convenient to operate.
6. Excessive use.
7. Good materials.
8. Good working order.
9. Good workmanship.
10. High quality.
11. In accordance with applicable published specifications.
12. In accordance with best commercial practice.
13. In accordance with best engineering practice.
14. Installed in a neat and workmanlike manner.
15. Metal parts shall be cleaned before painting.
16. Neatly finished.
17. Pleasing lines.
18. Practically free.
19. Properly assembled.
20. Rapid heating.
21. Reasonably clear.
22. Securely mounted.
23. Skillfully fitted.
24. Smooth surfaces.
25. Suitably finished.
26. Suitably housed.
27. To the satisfaction of the buyer.
28. Undesirable odor.
29. Where practical.
30. Within easy reach of the operator.
31. Workmanship shall be of the highest quality.

Appendix E

Description/Specification/ Work Statement

TABLE OF CONTENTS

Article No.	Article Name	Page No.
SOW.1	Scope	152
SOW.2	Applicable Documents	153
SOW.3	Requirements	155
SOW.4	Progress Reports	162

SOW.1 *SCOPE*

SOW.1.1 *GENERAL.* The Supplier shall provide all services and materials necessary to warehouse/store and fill orders for Buyer-provided educational materials by means of a combination firm-fixed-price and indefinite-quantity type contract.

SOW.1.2 *OBJECTIVE.* The services set forth in this Subcontract are those required to operate an educational material storage and distribution point for the Buyer. The Supplier shall perform all warehousing/storage and order-filling functions, to include receiving, processing, storing, inventory control, packaging, labeling, marking, and mailing of Buyer-provided materials.

SOW.1.3 *REQUIREMENTS.* Supplier operations shall be inclusive of the following detailed work requirements in specific tasks as specified in Section SOW.6. Requirements SOW.1.3.1 through SOW.1.3.5 below are considered warehousing/storage functions and are included in the firm-fixed-price portion of the Schedule (Item 0001). Requirements SOW.1.3.6 through SOW.1.3.10 are considered order-filling functions and are included in the indefinite-quantity portion of the Schedule (Items 0002A through 0002D).

SOW.1.3.1 Receive, unload, and in-check materials.

SOW.1.3.2 Hold and process discrepant material, that is, damages, overages, and shortages.

SOW.1.3.3 Perform item-by-item shipping documentation check.

SOW.1.3.4 Store and protect from damage and pilferage all educational materials.

SOW.1.3.5 Maintain inventory control system for materials.

SOW.1.3.6 Receive orders for shipment, either from the Buyer or the ultimate customers.

SOW.1.3.7 Package, mark, label, and mail individual orders.

SOW.1.3.8 Provide tracer research on orders not received by customers.

SOW.1.3.9 Assure quality control.

SOW.1.3.10 Provide reports.

SOW.1.4 *WORK SCHEDULE.* The Supplier shall receive and unload materials, including the receiving of postal mail, between 9 AM and 5 PM Monday through Friday. Order filling shall be confined to the same time period.

APPLICABLE DOCUMENTS

Table of Contents

Paragraph	Titles	Page No.
SOW.2	Applicable Documents	154
SOW.2.1	Buyer-Furnished Publications and Applicable Forms	154
SOW 2.2	Regulations	154

SOW.2 *APPLICABLE DOCUMENTS*

SOW.2.1 *BUYER FURNISHED PUBLICATIONS AND APPLICABLE FORMS.* The Supplier shall adhere to the policies and standards contained in Buyer-provided regulations, technical manuals, and other federal, state, local, and industrial publications. The Buyer will make the final determination regarding interpretation of governing publications. The Supplier may request publications by submitting a letter to the Technical Representative of the Buyer.

SOW.2.2 *REGULATIONS.*

Regulation	Date	Title
CFR 29-1910	1 Jul 88	Occupational Safety and Health Standard
CFR 49	1 Oct 86	Code of Federal Regulations 49 (Transportation)

REQUIREMENTS

Table of Contents

Paragraph	Titles
SOW.3	Requirements
SOW.3.1	Acronymns, Abbreviations, and Definitions
SOW.3.1.1	Acronyms and Abbreviations
SOW.3.1.2	Definitions
SOW.3.2	Buyer-Furnished Property and Services
SOW.3.2.1	General
SOW.3.2.2	Buyer-Furnished Materials
SOW.3.2.3	Inventory of Buyer Materials Upon Termination
SOW.3.2.4	Supplier Responsibility for Loss or Damage
SOW.3.2.5	Supplier Periodic Inventory of Materials
SOW.3.3	Supplier-Furnished Property and Services
SOW.3.3.1	General
SOW.3.4	Work Requirements
SOW.3.4.1	Specific Tasks
SOW.3.4.1.1	Receive, Unload, and In-check Materials
SOW.3.4.1.2	Hold and Process Discrepant Material, i.e., Damages, Overages, and Shortages
SOW.3.4.1.3	Perform Item-by-item Shipping Documentation Check
SOW.3.4.1.4	Store and Protect from Damage and Pilferage all Educational Materials
SOW.3.4.1.5	Maintain Inventory Control System for Materials
SOW.3.4.1.6	Receive Orders for Shipment, Either from the Buyer or the Ultimate Customers
SOW.3.4.1.7	Package, Mark, Label, and Mail Individual Orders
SOW.3.4.1.8	Provide Tracer Research on Orders Not Received
SOW.3.4.1.9	Assure Quality Control

SOW.3 *REQUIREMENTS*

SOW.3.1 *ACRONYMNS, ABBREVIATIONS, AND DEFINITIONS.* Acronyms, abbreviations, and definitions that may be used throughout the performance work statement and this Subcontract are listed below:

SOW.3.1.1 Acronyms and Abbreviations.

BFE	Buyer-Furnished Equipment	PS	Postal Service
BFM	Buyer-Furnished Material	PWS	Performance Work Statement
BFP	Buyer-Furnished Property	QA	Quality Assurance
CBL	Commercial Bill of Lading or Freight Bill	QC	Quality Control
CDR	Contract Discrepancy Report	RFP	Request for Proposal
COB	Close of Business	ROD	Report of Discrepancy
CY	Calendar Year	SFE	Supplier Furnished Equipment
EEO	Equal Employment Opportunity	SFM	Supplier Furnished Material
EPA	Environmental Protection Agency	SFP	Supplier Furnished Property
FOIA	Freedom of Information Act	SOP	Standard Operating Procedures
FY	Fiscal Year	SOSO	Supplier Owned-Supplier Operated
IAW	In Accordance With‘	TET	Technical Evaluation Team
NA	Not Applicable	TRB	Technical Representative of the Buyer
NLT	Not Later Than	UPS	United Parcel Service
OSHA	Occupational Safety and Health Act	USPO	United States Post Office
OST	Order Ship Time	USPS	United States Postal Service
POC	Point of Contact		

SOW.3.1.2 Definitions.

Bill of Lading, Commercial (CBL): A contract between the shipper and the carrier whereby the carrier agrees to furnish transportation service subject to the conditions printed on the reverse side of the bill of lading.

Bimonthly: Occurring every two months.

Calendar Days: Every day of the year including weekends and holidays. This includes 365 days in a year, 366 days in a leap year.

Consignee: The receiving person to whom the material is addressed or consigned, as indicated by the appropriate shipping/mailing document.

Consignor: The supplier facility from which shipment is made.

Contract Discrepancy Report: A formal written report, with documentation, initiated by the TRB and completed by the Supplier. Issued to the Supplier whenever performance is unsatisfactory.

Customer: The individual authorized to receive materials shipped by the Supplier.

Deficiency: An instance of noncompliance with subcontract requirements.

Hand Receipt: Document listing all items that have been issued from a property control activity to an individual.

His/Her: Wherever used in the PWS the term "his" is meant to be synonymous with "her" unless otherwise stated. The same shall be true for "he" and "she."

Inventory: A physical count of items located within the activity.

Operating Supplies: Supplies, forms, labels, tape, mailing containers, and so forth.

Performance Work Statement (PWS): A document that describes contractable work to be accomplished.

Quality Assurance: Those actions taken by the Buyer to evaluate services to determine that they meet the contractual requirements.

Quality Control: A method used by the Supplier to control the quality of services provided.

Services: Products (tangible or intangible) that are to be provided by the Supplier.

Standard: An acknowledged measure of comparison.

Standard Inspection Requirement: A requirement that the Supplier maintain an acceptable inspection system.

Buyer: The employee assigned to administer, approve, and control contracted work for the Buying firm.

Supplier: The Supplier and any of its subcontractors.

Supplier Representative: A person employed by or representing the Supplier.

Surveillance: The process of monitoring Supplier performance by direct evaluation or observation.

Technical Evaluation Team: The technical personnel responsible for evaluating offeror technical proposals and reporting their recommendations thereon to the Buyer.

Technical Representative of the Buyer (TRB): The Buying firm employee, as appointed by the Buyer, responsible for technical administration of the Subcontract.

SOW.3.2 *BUYER FURNISHED PROPERTY AND SERVICES.*

SOW.3..2.1 *GENERAL.*

SOW.3.2.1.1   The Buyer will furnish all educational materials to the Supplier.

SOW.3.2.1.2   The Buyer will furnish no facilities, utilities, equipment, communications, durables, or operating supplies to the Supplier.

SOW.3.2.2 *BUYER FURNISHED MATERIALS.* The following Buyer property shall be furnished to the Supplier on the Subcontract start date:

Item Description	Estimated Quantity
40×60 In. Charts	5,000
20×30 In. Charts	5,000
Binder Size Charts	2,000
Computer Diskettes, 3 ½″	2,000

SOW.3.2.3 *INVENTORY OF BUYER MATERIALS UPON TERMINA-TION.* The Supplier, the Supplier's designated property administrator, and the Technical Representative of the Buyer shall conduct a joint inventory of all Buyer furnished materials. This inventory shall be conducted prior to subcontract start date and again at subcontract termination. The Supplier and the TRB shall both certify that the inventory is correct with all discrepancies noted. Quantities listed in SOW.3.2 are firm only after a joint inventory has been conducted. If the Supplier does not participate in the inventory, the Supplier shall accept as accurate the listing of materials provided by Buyer.

SOW.3.2.4 *SUPPLIER RESPONSIBILITY FOR LOSS OR DAMAGE.* The Supplier shall be liable for loss or damage to contractor furnished materials, beyond fair wear and tear IAW the provision of this Subcontract entitled "Buyer-Property, Furnished by the Buyer." Compensation will be determined by the Buyer with direct payment from the Supplier. In the case of damaged or lost materials, the amount of compensation due the Buyer by the Supplier shall be the actual cost of replacement.

SOW.3.2.5 *SUPPLIER PERIODIC INVENTORY OF MATERIALS.* The Supplier shall complete an end of the month inventory of all materials on the last working day of each month. A report shall be submitted to the TRB not later than the end of the 3rd working day of the following month on the inventory status.

SOW.3.3 *SUPPLIER FURNISHED PROPERTY AND SERVICES.*

SOW.3.3.1 *GENERAL.* Supplier shall furnish all management, supervision, personnel, labor, transportation, facilities, utilities, equipment, office supplies, operating supplies, tools, parts, clothing, and communications to accomplish work requirements. The only exception to this shall be the Buyer-provided education materials.

SOW.3.4 *WORK REQUIREMENTS.* The Supplier shall assure that all subcontract work requirements are accomplished IAW subcontract specifications. The Supplier shall monitor all work as described in Section E, paragraph E.3.

SOW.3.4.1 *SPECIFIC TASKS.* Tasks SOW.3.4.1.1 through 3.4.1.5 are considered warehousing/storage services and relate to Line Item 0001 of Schedule B of this Contract. These services shall be continuously provided and paid for on a firm-fixed-price (lump sum) basis per month. Tasks SOW.3.4.1.6 through SOW.3.4.1.9 are considered order-filling services and relate to Line Items 0002A, 0002B, 0002C, and 0002D of Schedule B of this Contract. These services shall be ordered as needed and paid for on a fixed unit price basis, with payment at the end of the month based on orders filled.

SOW.3.4.1.1 Receive, Unload, and In-Check Materials. The Supplier shall unload and in-check materials received. The Supplier shall annotate the shipping invoice with the number of pieces received and date unloaded.

SOW.3.4.1.2 Hold and Process Discrepant Material, that is, Damages, Overages, and Shortages. The Supplier shall sign the shipping document and confirm overages, shortages, and damages by annotating the discrepancies on the receiving document. The carrier's signature is obtained as verification of material discrepancies. Discrepancies will be certified by the TRB.

SOW.3.4.1.3 Perform Item-by-Item Shipping Documentation Check. The Supplier will verify each piece of material received against the shipping documents to assure accuracy.

SOW.3.4.1.4 Store and Protect From Damage and Pilferage all Educational Materials. All educational materials are considered highly pilferable items and shall be placed in a secure area. In addition, they are of a fragile nature and easily damaged. The Supplier shall exercise due care to insure materials are not damaged. Items damaged or stolen while in the possession of the Supplier shall be replaced at cost at the Supplier's expense.

SOW.3.4.1.5 Maintain Inventory Control System for Materials.

SOW.3.4.1.5.1 Offerors shall be required to submit a written explanation of their standard commercial inventory control systems to the Buyer as part of their technical proposals.

SOW.3.4.1.5.2 The Supplier shall manage buyer-provided educational materials in accordance with the standard commercial practices divulged in his technical proposal.

SOW.3.4.1.6 Receive Orders for Shipment, Either from the buyer or the Ultimate Customers. The Supplier shall be prepared to receive orders for materials by telephone or mail either from the buyer or from the ultimate customers.

SOW.3.4.1.7 Package, Mark, Label, and Mail Individual Orders. The Supplier shall package, wrap, box, or otherwise protect the materials in transit. Packaging materials shall be chosen so as to ease handling within the Supplier facility and at final destination. The Supplier shall mark and label all shipments with the following return address:

    _____

    _____

    _____

The address label will reflect the customer's complete name, address, city, state, and zip code. The mailing label shall clearly indicate 4th class mail (educational materials). Shipment will be via USPS at 4th class rates.

SOW.3.4.1.8 Provide Tracer Research on Orders not Received by Customers. The Supplier shall keep a daily order log of all materials shipped in order to respond to requests from the buyer to conduct tracer research on orders not received by customers.

SOW.3.4.1.9 Assure Quality Control. The Supplier is responsible for controlling the quality of contract services and for ensuring that services conform to contractual requirements. The Supplier shall provide and maintain an inspection system acceptable to the buyer covering the services under this Contract. Complete records of all inspection work performed by the Supplier shall be maintained and made available to the buyer during contract performance. The Supplier's standard inspection requirements shall be made a part of the technical proposal and shall be updated as changes occur.

PROGRESS REPORTS

TABLE OF CONTENTS

Paragraph	Titles	Page No.
SOW.4	Progress Reports	163
SOW.4.1	Inventory Received Report	163
SOW.4.2	Periodic Inventory Report	163
SOW.4.3	Items Shipped Report	163

SOW.4 *PROGRESS REPORTS*

SOW.4.1 *INVENTORY RECEIVED REPORT.* The Supplier shall submit to the TRB a list of items received by item description and quantity not later than 12:00 AM the day after receipt.

SOW.4.2 *PERIODIC INVENTORY REPORT.* The Supplier or shall submit to the TRB a periodic inventory report as of the last working day of each month. The report shall include for each category of material the ending inventory for the previous month, items received from the buyer during the month, items shipped during the month, and final inventory. This report shall be submitted to the TRB not later than the 3rd working day of the following month.

SOW.4.3 *ITEMS SHIPPED REPORT.* As part of its monthly invoice, the Supplier shall submit a list of items shipped by category. This report shall constitute the basis for paying the Contractor for Line Items 0002A, 0002B, 0002C, and 0002D of the Contract.

Appendix F

Example Request for Quotation

NAME OF ORGANIZATION ISSUING THE SOLICITATION

(ABBREVIATION)

REQUEST FOR QUOTATION

RFQ NO. _____

Firm Name	Mail Quotation To: **Buyer Organization** **Street Name and Number** Box or Mail Stop City, State and Zip Code ATTN: Buyer's Name
Street	
City, State, Zip Code, Phone	Mark Envelope "Do not Open - RFQ No._____
	Your bid may be faxed in lieu of the above.
_____ _____ Authorized Signature Date	

ISSUED UNDER CONTRACT NO. _____   WITH _____

Date Issued	Quote Due By	Delivery Required	Page	Refer Questions To: Buyer's Name
			1 of _	Phone: Fax:

Item	Quantity	Unit	Description	Unit Price	Ext. Price
			This is a Request for Quotation (RFQ) issued by (Name of Organization). Please quote your net prices, after applicable discounts, for the item(s) listed. See pages two and three for the items to be quoted. Please read this RFQ and all attachments carefully, and complete all information in the spaces provided on this page, on pages 2 & 3, and on the Representations and Certifications. Please submit these completed documents as well as a Technical Proposal. See Instructions to Offerors. For traceability purposes, the invoice on any resultant contract stemming from this solicitation must directly correlate to the items on the contract.		

Payment Terms:	FOB / Shipping Point:	Total Quoted Price For All Items: $

NAME OF ORGANIZATION ISSUING THE SOLICITATION

(ABBREVIATION)

REQUEST FOR QUOTATION

CONTRACT LINE ITEMS

A.   Offerors shall enter unit prices and amounts for contract line items and subline items in the schedules that follow.

B.   In the event there is a difference between a unit price and the extended total amount, the unit price will be held to be the intended offer and the total recomputed accordingly.   If the offeror provides a total amount for a contract item but fails to enter the unit price, the amount divided by the specified quantity will be held to be the intended unit price.

SCHEDULE OF FIRM-FIXED-PRICE SERVICES

SCHEDULE					
Item				Unit	
No.	Supplies/Services	Quantity	Unit	Price	Amount

0001 Review documentation submitted by the buyer in order to complete a report and render an opinion. The Supplier's work under the firm-fixed-price Line Item 0001 portion of the contract shall be considered complete when the final report has been submitted to the buyer not later than _____. (See Paragraph 1.2.1, Statement of Work).

0001A Final Report and Opinion   1   Ea   ____ $_____
      by _____

TOTAL PRICE FOR CONTRACT   X X   X X   X X $_____
(LINE ITEM 0001)

NAME OF ORGANIZATION ISSUING THE SOLICITATION

(ABBREVIATION)

REQUEST FOR QUOTATION

RFQ NO. _____

PAGE 3 OF 5

0002 Prepare documentation, drawings, and artwork necessary and appropriate to the completion of the work. This work shall be completed prior to _____. (See Paragraph 1.2.2, Statement of Work).

0002A Completion of Documentation,   1 Ea   ____ $_____
      Drawings, and Artwork by _____

TOTAL PRICE FOR CONTRACT   X X   X X   X X $_____
    (LINE ITEM 0002)

SCHEDULE OF TIME-AND-MATERIALS SERVICES

SCHEDULE Item No.	Supplies/Services	Estimated Quantity	Unit	Unit Price	Amount

0003 Provide Professional Services subsequent to completion of documentation, drawings, and artwork and provide continuing services for a three year period commencing upon notice of award. (See Paragraph 1.2.3, Statement of Work)

0003A Professional Hours   500 HRS ____ $_____

0003B Materials At Cost (ESTIMATED)   XX XX X X $10,000.00

TOTAL PRICE FOR CONTRACT   XX X X   X X $_____
    (LINE ITEM 0003)

TOTAL PRICE FOR CONTRACT   X X X X   X X X X X X $_____
    (LINE ITEMS 0001, 0002, and 0003)

NAME OF ORGANIZATION ISSUING THE SOLICITATION

(ABBREVIATION)

REQUEST FOR QUOTATION

RFQ NO. _____
PAGE 4 OF 5

I.   GENERAL INFORMATION

It is the intention of this solicitation to obtain professional services to complete certain clearly defined work tasks and provide continuing professional services for a three year period commencing upon receipt of notice of award. The buyer reserves the right to award one contract for Line Items 0001 and 0002 and to award one or more contracts for continuing professional services in Line Item 0003. Quotations must be submitted on this form in triplicate, and returned to the address as shown in the upper right hand corner of Page 1. If so specified herein by the buyer, quotations may be faxed in lieu of the above. Quotations are due by the close-of-business on the date indicated. However, the buyer reserves the right to consider a later proposal if deemed to be in the best interest of the buyer. This solicitation does not commit the buyer to pay for any costs incurred in the preparation or submission of any quotation or to procure the services hereunder. Any offers accompanied by terms and conditions essentially different from the enclosed referenced terms and conditions may be considered unacceptable.

II.   DELIVERY

The buyer's required completion date for Line Item 0001 is _____. The buyer's required completion for Line 0002, is _____. If you cannot meet these dates, indicate the best dates you can meet in the following spaces: Line Item 0001: _____; Line Item 0002: _____. Please do not quote to a completion date you cannot meet. All offerors will be contractually committed to the quoted date upon issuance of any contract. The buyer reserves the right to consider as non-responsive all bids with completion dates later than the aforementioned required completion date.

III.   REQUEST FOR QUOTATION - INSTRUCTIONS TO OFFERORS

Offeror's attention is directed to the attached "Instructions to Offerors", which are made a part of this solicitation.

IV.   REPRESENTATIONS AND CERTIFICATIONS

Offerors must complete and return the Representations and Certifications Form, as provided herein, with their quotation.

NAME OF ORGANIZATION ISSUING THE SOLICITATION

(ABBREVIATION)

REQUEST FOR QUOTATION

RFQ NO. _____
PAGE 5 OF 5

V.   OFFER VALIDITY PERIOD

In compliance with the above, the offeror agrees, if this quotation be accepted within sixty (60) calendar days from the quote due date, to furnish any or all of the items upon which prices are quoted, at the price set opposite each item, delivered at the designated points within the time frame specified.

VI.   TERMS AND CONDITIONS AND OTHER DOCUMENTS

The following items are attached and are made a part of this Request for Quotation:

(a)   Terms & Conditions for Fixed-Price Service Contracts.   (Applicable to Line Items 0001 and 0002 only).

(b)   Terms and Conditions for Time and Material/Labor Hour Service Contracts,. (Applicable to Line Item 0003 only).

(c)   Specimen Contract

(d)   Instructions to Offerors.

(e)   Representations, Certifications & Other Statements of Offerors.

(f)   Description/Specification/Work Statement

Appendix G

Example Contract Agreement

SUBCONTRACT AGREEMENT

WITH

This CONTRACT AGREEMENT entered into as of the ___ day of _____,
199_ between _____., (herein called "THE
COMPANY"), and _____, with offices at _____, (herein
called "SUPPLIER"). The attached sections I-V form the basis for this
agreement.

   I.   Parties to the Agreement

   II.   General Objectives

   III.   Contract Type

   IV.   Agreements

   V   Signature Block

CONTRACT AGREEMENT

I. **Parties to the Agreement**

_____. (THE COMPANY)

_____ (SUPPLIER)

II. **General Objectives**

This Contract is made for the procurement of services needed in connection
with the Company's _____.

III. **Contract Type**

This Contract is a labor hour type contract.

IV. **Agreements**

1. S c o p e : Provide services with respect to the activities at
_____ including, but not limited to:

_____.

_____.

_____.

2. **Effective   Date:**   The effective date of this agreement is
_____.

3. **Completion   Date:**   The completion date of this agreement is
_____.

4. **Hourly Rate(s):** An hourly rate of $____ will be charged irrespective of
the billing rate normally charged by the Supplier. This hourly rate includes
all labor, benefits, materials, overhead, secretarial/clerical services, general
and administrative costs, and all other costs except copying, postage, word
processing, long distance telephone/telefax charges, and travel. It is
expected that the Supplier will be performing work while on travel;
provided, however, the maximum daily payment on travel days shall not
exceed eight hours.

5. **Ceiling Price:** The total price of this Contract shall not exceed
$_____.

6. **Invoices:** Applications for payment in the form of invoices may be
submitted not more frequently than monthly. Invoices shall reference the
contract number and be mailed, in triplicate, to:

Mr. _____
_____
_____

7. **Supplier Acquired Property:** There shall be no property purchased by
the Supplier as an item of allowable cost hereunder.

8. **Travel Expenses:** Allowable costs for travel shall be in accordance with
the Company's travel policy.

Contract Agreement #_____
Page 2

    9. Contract Contents: There is hereby incorporated the following:

        a.   General Provisions, Contract # _____.

    10. Entire Agreement. This Contract contains the entire understanding between the parties, and there are no understandings or representations not set forth or incorporated by reference herein. No subsequent modifications of this Contract shall be of any force or effect unless in writing signed by the parties claimed to be bound hereby. No communications, written or oral, by other than the buyer shall be effective to modify or otherwise affect the provisions of this Contract.

V. Signature Block

    The undersigned have executed this Contract Agreement as of the date indicated above.

for _____ (THE COMPANY)

_____

for the SUPPLIER (_____)

_____

Appendix H

The Contract Administration Team

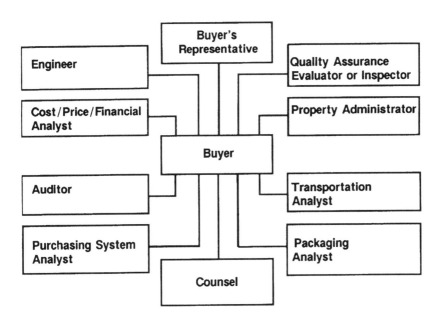

Appendix I

Work Order and Payment Procedures Flow Chart for an Indefinite-Delivery Type Contract

WORK ORDER AND PAYMENT PROCEDURES FLOW CHART FOR AN INDEFINITE DELIVERY TYPE CONTRACT

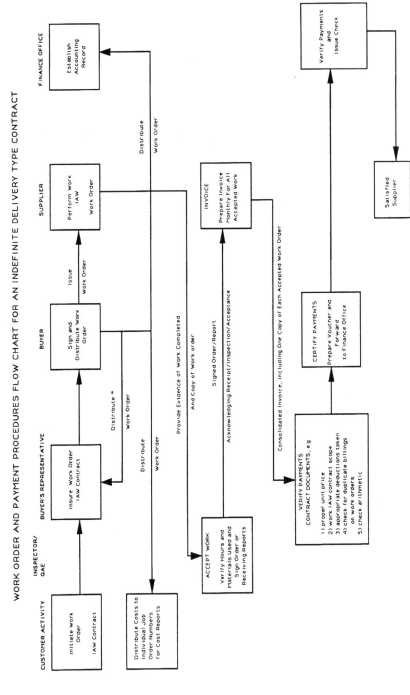

178

Appendix J

Contract Closeout Checklist

Contract No. _____ Report No. _____ Month _____

Supplier _____ Cost Code(s) _____

Contract Title _____ Area _____

Type of Contract _____ Current Status _____

<table>
<tr><th>AMOUNT</th><th>DATE</th></tr>
<tr><td>Award: _____</td><td>Award:_____</td></tr>
<tr><td>Modifications: _____</td><td>Original CCD:_____</td></tr>
<tr><td>Total Contract: _____</td><td>Revised CCD:_____</td></tr>
<tr><td>Assessed LDs: _____</td><td>BOD:_____</td></tr>
<tr><td>Supplier NET: _____</td><td>Punch List Complete:_____</td></tr>
</table>

CLOSE OUT ACTIVITY	*STATUS	DATE
1. Supplier's Notice of Completion	_____	_____
2. Outstanding Requirements Letter	_____	_____
Input Received From		
- Project	_____	_____
- Construction		
- Construction Manager	_____	_____
- Area Superintendent/Manager	_____	_____
- Engineering	_____	_____
- Vendor Information Control	_____	_____
- Inspection/Quality Control	_____	_____
- Cost/Scheduling	_____	_____
- Accounts Payable	_____	_____
- Contracts		
- Project/Jobsite	_____	_____
- Program Office	_____	_____
3. All Work Orders Finalized	_____	_____
4. All Contract Modifications Finalized	_____	_____
5. All Contract Modifications Fully Executed	_____	_____
6. Claims Backcharges, and All Problems Resolved	_____	_____
7. Contract Value and Payment Log Reconciled	_____	_____
8. Notice of Rejection	_____	_____

Note: If Notice of Rejection issued, attach this checklist to new checklist and repeat cycle as appropriate.

* R - Received   I - Issued   W - Waived
  C - Completed   T - Transmitted   N/A - Not Applicable

CONTRACT CLOSE OUT
CHECKLIST (CONTINUED)

9.   Notice of Acceptance   _____   _____
     The Buyer's Technical Representative and Project Manager or
     his designee will approve all final technical acceptances.
10. Certification and Release   _____   _____
     All final as-built drawings must be certified with appropriate
     civil engineer seals!!
11. Items Normally Required from the Supplier
     at Final Acceptance:
                    - Outstanding Submittals   _____   _____
                    - List of Installed Equipment   _____   _____
                    - As-Built List of Materials   _____   _____
                    - Tabulation of Testing   _____   _____
                    - Special Guarantees/Warranties for
                         Spares/Parts/Deliverables   _____   _____
                    - Finish Items   _____   _____
                    - Keys   _____   _____
                    - Test/Special Equipment/Tools   _____   _____
                    - Mechanical Items   _____   _____
                    - Electrical Items   _____   _____
                    - Operation/Maintenance/Instr Manuals _____   _____
12. Transmittal Letter for 9. and 10.   _____   _____
13. Training Sessions Scheduled and User Notified   _____   _____
14. a. Prefinal (Renewable Parts Replaced) to determine
              readiness for usable completion   _____   _____
     b. Equipment Serial Numbers Checked Against Documentation
                                                          _____   _____
     c. Buyer-Furnished or Supplier-Acquired Property
                                                          _____   _____
15. a. User Prefinal Scheduled   _____   _____
     b. Prefinal Comments Received   _____   _____
16. User Contacted to Arrange Special Inspections and
              Certification   _____   _____
17. Surplus/Salvage/Extras Disposition Determined   _____   _____
18. Warranties, Safety Precautions, Operating Instructions, and
              Postings Verified   _____   _____
19. Certified As-Built Drawings plus All Shop Drawings Related to
              Changes and Claims Received   _____   _____
20. a. Beneficial Occupancy Inspection   _____   _____
     b. Interested Parties Informed of BOD Acceptance_____   _____
21. a. Completion Photos and Video Tapes Requested_____   _____
     b. Completion Photos Provided   _____   _____

* R - Received   I - Issued   W - Waived
  C - Completed   T - Transmitted   N/A - Not Applicable

CONTRACT CLOSE OUT
CHECKLIST (CONTINUED)

22. Custody Transfer (turnover) Letter to User (w/enclosures)
   - Acceptance Letter and Punchlist   ----------   ----------
   - As-Built Drawings   ----------   ----------
   - Submittals   ----------   ----------
   - Warranty/Performance Period   ----------   ----------
   - Schedules   ----------   ----------
   - Others   ----------   ----------
23. a. Punchlist Correction Inspection   ----------   ----------
    b. Punchlist Correction Verification Lettter to Supplier
                                                ----------   ----------
24. Final Payrolls and Labor Provisions Received and Verified
                                                                  ----
25. Property Pass Books Returned to Facility Security Office,
       (if appropriate)   ----------   ----------
26. Supplier's Final Invoice
   - Invoice in Required Format/Amount   ----------   ----------
   - Notice of Acceptance   ----------   ----------
   - Certification and Release   ----------   ----------
27. Return/Release of Performance and Payment Bonds by
       Purchasing Manager   ----------   ----------
28. Final Invoice Approvals   ----------   ----------
29. Final Invoice to Accounts Payable   ----------   ----------
30. Final Payment to Supplier   ----------   ----------
31. Contract Close Out Report   ----------   ----------
32. Notice to Supplier   ----------   ----------
33. Supplier Performance Evaluation   ----------   ----------
34. All Close Out Documentation in File   ----------   ----------

* R - Received   I - Issued   W - Waived
  C - Completed   T - Transmitted   N/A - Not Applicable

Index

Advance payments. *See* Payments
Advance purchasing plan, 14, 17, 19, 20, 22, 65, 75
Annual work plan (AWP), 93–94
Assignment of claims, 115
Awarding the service contract, 82
  contracts requiring bonding, 82, 85
  dealing with unsuccessful offerors, 83
  distributing contract copies, 83
  documenting supplier acceptance, 82

Bonding requirements, 6, 11, 15

Claims. *See* Supplier claims
Closing out contracts, 131
Competitive bidding, 61
Competitive range, 65, 67–68, 75
Contract administration, 10, 13, 39, 87
  annual work plan, 93–94
  buyer's representative's responsibilities, 88–90
  buyer's responsibilities, 88
  contract administration plan, 91–92, 116
  contract administration team, 88, 91–92, 96–98, 102, 110, 115
  financial administration of contracts, 87, 107
  incrementally funded contracts, 95, 108, 110–11
  notice to proceed, 83–85, 93–95
  objectives, 87
  ordering and work authorization, 93–95, 116
  payments. *See* Payments *and* Contract payments
  QA evaluator/inspector responsibilities, 90–91
  routine vs. non-routine, 87
  work authorizations, 93–94, 116

Contract changes, 88, 90–91, 95–97, 100–2, 116–17
administrative changes, 96–97, 116
cardinal changes, 96, 116
constructive changes, 96–98, 100–3, 117
change order, 89, 96–98, 100–3, 105, 116
changes outside the scope of the contract, 96, 102–5, 113, 116
changes provision—explained, given, analyzed, 96–97, 100–3, 105, 117
equitable adjustment. *See* Equitable adjustment
supplemental agreement. *See* Supplemental agreement
Contract closeout. *See* Closing out contracts
Contract modifications, 87–90, 94–97, 100, 103–5, 111, 116
bilateral, 98, 116
equitable adjustment. *See* Equitable adjustment
supplemental agreement. *See* Supplemental agreement
unilateral, 96–97, 99, 100, 102–3, 116
Contract payments, 111
payment authorization by contract type, 111
types of payments, 113–15, 117–18
Contract types, 10, 13, 15, 19, 20, 22–23, 27, 31, 93, 107, 111, 116
blanket order, 11, 33, 35, 38–39, 40
combination contracts, 33, 35, 44–45, 48

cost reimbursement, 13, 33, 40, 42–43, 47, 93–95, 108
administration of, 93, 95, 107–8, 111–13, 116
cost no-fee/cost sharing, 42, 47
cost-plus-award-fee, 43, 47
cost-plus-fixed-fee, 42, 47
cost-plus-incentive-fee, 42–43, 47
cost-plus-percentage-of-cost, 33, 44
firm-fixed-price, 10, 27, 33–35, 37, 44–46, 53, 61, 71, 93, 104, 107–8, 111, 117
fixed-price incentive, 34–35, 47
fixed-price with economic price adjustment, 33–34, 47
hybrid contracts, 43, 48
indefinite-delivery type, 27, 33, 35, 38–40, 44, 47
administration of, 90, 93, 116
indefinite quantity–indefinite delivery, 10, 13, 35–36, 41, 47, 54–55
requirements, 10–11, 35, 37–41, 44, 47, 53–54
time-and-material/labor hour, 10–11, 28, 33, 35, 43–45, 48
administration of, 93, 113, 116–17
Control points and milestones, 19–20, 22–23, 29, 94–95
Cost analysis, 62–64, 68, 74, 78–79, 84
when to employ, 63
Cost overrun, 107, 110

Definitions—Technical provision, 26
Differences between supply and service purchasing, 5–6, 13, 15

Disallowing costs (cost reimbursement contract), 108, 113
Disputes, 119, 123, 127–30
Economic price adjustment, 12, 19, 33–34, 47
Equitable adjustment, 97, 99–103
Evaluating supplier performance. See Supplier performance evaluation

Fact-finding, 77–78, 84
Final payment. See Payments
Financial administration of contracts, 107
    cost control by contract type, 107–8

Labor laws
    Contract Work Hours and Safety Standards Act (CWHSSA), 6, 8
    Davis-Bacon Act, 6, 9
    Fair Labor Standards Act (FLSA), 6, 8
    Service Contract Act (SCA), 6, 8
    Walsh-Healey Public Contracts Act, 6, 8
Limitation of Cost/Funds provision(s), 95, 108–10, 113
List of known suppliers, 18, 20

Make-or-buy decision, 18, 20
Monitoring supplier costs, 108–9

Negotiation, 77
    negotiating changes, 96–99

negotiation conference, 77–78, 80, 85
    negotiation documentation, 77, 80, 85
    steps in the negotiation process, 77, 84
Notice to proceed (NTP), 83–85

Partial payments. See Payments
Payments, types of. See also Financial Administration of Contracts
    advance payments, 108, 114, 118
    final payments, 108, 114–15, 118
    partial payments, 108, 114, 118
    progress payments, 108, 114, 118
Penalties for non-conformance, 6, 12, 15
Personal services, 2, 4, 10–11, 14, 20–22
Pre-negotiation memorandum, 77, 79–80, 84
Pre-negotiation review, 77–78, 84
Price analysis, 62, 64, 68–69, 71, 74–75, 77, 79, 81, 84
    methodologies, 62
    when to employ, 62
Price competition, 4, 7, 18, 20, 23, 63–65, 68, 72, 74–75
Procurement method, 19–20, 23, 61–62
Professional services, 2–5, 14, 19
Progress payments. See Payments

Quality requirements, 12–13, 28–29, 35, 42–43, 46, 61, 66

Renewal options, 12, 19, 89, 105–6, 117

Reports required of the supplier, 25–26, 28–29
Risk, 18–19, 31–33, 37–38, 40, 42, 47–48, 70, 73

Schedule of prices (contract schedule), 9, 12–13, 27, 36–37, 41, 49, 50, 53–55, 60
Scope of the work, 18, 25–26, 28, 44
Service, 1
Small-small/disadvantaged business setasides, 5–6, 15, 18, 20, 22, 31, 59
Sole-source, 7, 18–20, 23
Solicitation, 6, 10, 13–15, 18–20, 22, 26, 35, 37, 39, 44, 49, 62, 63–67, 75
  elements, 49
  purposes, 49, 59
Specimen contract, 49–50
Statements of work (SOW), 6, 9, 11–15, 25, 32–33, 39, 49–50, 60–61
  achieving clarity, 28–29
  common errors, 28–29
  major planning steps, 26–27
  major preparation steps, 26–27
  major sections, 25–26
Supplemental agreements, 97, 103–5, 116
Supplier acceptance (documentation of), 82
Supplier claims, 119
  claims avoidance, 120–21, 128
  defense against, 121–22, 128
  resolution of, 120–23
  situations leading to, 119–20, 122
  subcontractor claims against the supplier, 125–26, 129

Supplier performance evaluations, 131–32
Supplier selection, 6, 10, 17, 19–20, 22, 61
  "best value" source selection, 61, 64–68, 75
  competitive range, 65, 67–68, 75, 77, 84
  criteria, 6, 8, 10, 19, 61, 64–66, 74–75
  price/cost/business proposals, 61, 65–66, 68, 75
  rating proposals, 66–67, 74
  technical/management proposals, 61, 65–70, 74–75
  using non-price criteria, 64–65, 75
  using price/cost criteria, 61–64, 74

Terminations, 119, 124–27
  alternatives to termination, 124, 127–28
  cause/default, for 126–27, 130
  complete termination, 124, 127
  convenience, for 124–26, 129
  mutual cancellation, 124, 127, 129
  notice of termination, 124–26, 129
  partial termination, 124
  procedures for, 124–25, 129
  temporary work stoppage, 124
  termination inventory, 124–26, 129
Terms of performance, 4, 12–13, 17, 20, 22, 31–32, 43, 46, 49–50, 59–60
  clauses for standard terms
    continuity of services, 52
    delay of work, 57
    indefinite quantity, 54
    inspection of services, 50

key personnel, 51
ordering, 53
order limitations, 53
renewal (extension) option, 55
requirements, 54
stop work order, 57
suspension of work, 56
warranty of services, 58

Work authorizations, 93–95, 116
Work breakdown structure, 27, 29,
    36, 66
Work cost estimate, 17, 20, 22, 36,
    42, 45, 62–63, 70–71, 73–74
  in-house estimate, 6, 9, 15, 70
Work or Services Excluded
    provision, 25